BLOODY BRITISH HISTORY
SALISBURY

T0347449

BLOODY BRITISH HISTORY
HISTORY

SALISBURY

DAVID J. VAUGHAN

To Claire, my wife, who makes all things possible

First published in 2014

The History Press
The Mill, Brimscombe Port
Stroud, Gloucestershire, GL5 2QG
www.thehistorypress.co.uk

Reprinted in 2017

British Library Cataloguing in Publication Data.
A catalogue record for this book is available from the British Library.

ISBN 978 0 7509 5841 7

Typesetting and origination by The History Press
Printed in Great Britain

CONTENTS

INTRODUCTION

SALISBURY HAS KNOWN two incarnations. First it was at Old Sarum, a fortified settlement complete with castle and cathedral on the former Iron Age hill fort known in Saxon times as Searobyrg. Then, from 1220 and with the church breaking away from the royal garrison, New Salisbury rose up on land at Myrifield, its present site, with its majestic cathedral one of the most iconic in the world. So Salisbury, with its record-breaking spire and its status as the only city in Wiltshire, soon became one of the largest provincial centres in England.

Yet with its growth came grief – illness, war, accident, murder – and so much death. Travel now through the madness, mayhem and sin in the history of this remarkable place, from prehistory to the twentieth century – some eight millennia! Specific venues appear more than once, such was their import in Salisbury's past; others emerge out of the old neighbourhood: Fisherton, Wilton and Milford; while there will always be the Plain to the north. Along the way we will even reach the New World ... for a time only. But what a time!

David J. Vaughan, 2014

ACKNOWLEDGEMENTS

HUGE THANKS ARE due to Cate Ludlow at The History Press for her help, support and guidance during the writing of this book. Thanks also to my friends whom I still miss at the Wiltshire and Swindon History Centre – a world-class resource – in particular Claire Skinner, Michael Marshman and Steve Hobbs. To Adrian Green at Salisbury and South Wiltshire Museum, Richard Osgood, Senior Archaeologist at Defence Infrastructure Organisation (MOD), Martin Brown of WYSG (formerly of DIO) and last but not least, to the number of excellent resources on the history of Salisbury and its people, including salisburyinquests.wordpress.com and the work of John Chandler. Thank you all.

Every effort has been made to identify and contact copyright holders of the images used in the book. All queries should be addressed to the author c/o The History Press.

4000–1450 BC
BRING IN YOUR DEAD

Salisbury's Prehistory

IN THE EARLY to middle Neolithic, around 4000–3000 BC, there was no such thing as social order. Everyone was equal, in death as in life. There were no individual graves to visit, instead the dead were laid out on platforms or biers where the birds and dogs picked over the skin, tearing muscle from sinew and leaving clean, brilliant white bones. This excarnation was just the beginning. Particular bones, such as the skull, arms and legs, were carried ceremoniously into the long barrows we still see today and there set within the stone chambers inside. Now they joined others bone with bone, so that no one individual remained whole. These public tombs were not just for memory, they were a link to the ancestors.

One such, to the north-east of Salisbury, Fussell's Lodge is the long barrow par excellence. The entire structure, including the massive earthen mound which today often remains the only visible element, was built between 3800 and 3600 BC. Here, disarticulated bones of up to fifty-seven individuals were left within the barrow, a huge number. But what makes this particular example even more impressive is that it contained a mortuary house: a timber structure where the bodies were defleshed and other funeral rites carried out. This was where the dead and living – the body and the soul – were separated: the flesh stripped from the bones and the spirit free to leave as a result. The once 'polluting' corpse had

Entrance to West Kennet long barrow. (David J. Vaughan)

WHY ONE DEAD BODY IS GREATER
THAN THE SUM OF ITS PARTS

Although articulated bodies were often interred in Neolithic long barrows, it was the round barrows of the Bronze Age that focused attention on the dead individual, rather than the assembled body parts of the many.

This was the age of hierarchy. Beneath each barrow, an individual, important for some political or cultural reason long since lost, was laid in the grave in a crouched position, with goods to accompany them into the afterlife, rich with symbolic meaning. The barrow or mound was cast upwards as a monumental covering; but it was not the last time the barrow would be used.

Arguably the most important near Salisbury is Bush Barrow, still standing proudly topped by the singular shrub that explains its name. Inside lay some of the earliest metalwork known in Britain, including two gold lozenge plates, bronze daggers, one studded with 140,000 gold pins, each thinner than a human hair; bone pins, the highly polished head of a stone or fossil mace and a bronze axe. For the first time, the collection can now be seen in the Wiltshire Heritage Museum, Devizes.

In most round-barrow burials, the body itself is unharmed, bearing no sign of trauma, injury, sacrifice or ritual murder. These were the revered dead, those members of society who led and inspired many. Unlike many of their Neolithic counterparts, they travelled into the next life whole and intact, their decaying physical form now as sacred as their soul had always been.

been made into a revered – and not to be feared – ancestor.

A similar yet different type of long barrow once stood north of Old Sarum, east of Castle Hill. In a tantalising twist on the timber mortuary enclosure at Fussell's Lodge, there are signs here of one having been built in stone. The thoughts behind this choice of material have been lost in time, yet such things were no accident.

Travelling farther north, along the road to Airman's Cross, you reach the modern A303. Here lies Long Barrow – an example so special it needed no other name, which it shares with the nearby modern roundabout.

In many cases, these communal tombs were used again in the Bronze Age

(*see* text box). But now the bodies were of individual people, no longer stripped of their flesh but buried whole. Discovered within the gigantic mound of Long Barrow were the remains of some seven complete skeletons, all male, crouched and intact. These secondary burials almost certainly date to between 1800 and 1450 BC.

At Normanton Down, on the other side of the present road, yet another long mound contained later, articulated inhumations. These four were strangely placed though, huddled together on the very floor of the barrow, a new family of the dead when the mound was raised.

A short distance further east is Ende Burgh (Saxon for 'Hands Barrow'). This is a special monument, confusingly

A long barrow with its earth and stone mound removed in antiquity. (David J. Vaughan)

interpreted as either a single Neolithic long barrow or two, possibly even three, round barrows from the Bronze Age. When superficially investigated in antiquity, human bones were discovered scattered across the mound(s), evidence of an even earlier investigation or perhaps, more likely, the now familiar Neolithic selection process of burying just the long bones and the skulls. Yet this was not the end of Ende Burgh. A further excavation in 1941 revealed two Saxon inhumations, whole as in the Bronze Age but now given a much later date. Hence, its Saxon name has stuck. Whatever its true age, this place on earth was, for such a long time, somewhere the dead could rest ...

In 1976, archaeologists working in the main ditch at Stonehenge, the prehistoric monument to top them all, unexpectedly unearthed a male skeleton buried in around 2300 BC. He was immediately dubbed the Stonehenge Archer due to the wrist guard and arrowheads found lying against his body. To their astonishment, the investigators realised the latter had lost their tips, which they found soon after embedded deep within the man's ribcage. No ordinary burial, then. A murdered enemy? This archer had suffered a violent death, shot at close range and buried in the ditch. But why here, at this site of such sanctity? Could he have been a sacrifice?

Whether in honour of the ancestors, to appease the gods or cleanse the world of the polluting dead, the dear departed in prehistory were revered, as important to those left behind as they are to us today when we visit their graves. There is nothing new in the world, only the old ways, rediscovered.

3000 BC–AD 700

LIFE AND DEATH AT STONEHENGE

Healing, Sacrifice and Ritual

IN THE YEAR of the new and long-awaited visitor centre at Airman's Cross, no book about Salisbury's dark history would be complete without a trip to Stonehenge. From healing to killing, festivals to murder, this stone circle has seen it all. But let's begin with a more peaceful side: its declared ability to heal the sick.

In the twelfth century, Geoffrey of Monmouth recorded:

> For in these stones is a mystery, and a healing virtue against many ailments … for they washed the stones and poured the water into baths, whereby those who were sick were cured. Moreover, they mixed confections of herbs with the water, whereby those who were wounded were healed, for not a stone is there that is wanting in virtue or leechcraft.

Five centuries later, John Aubrey, the king's antiquarian, was more succinct, if not fanciful: 'pieces (or powder) of these stones putt into their Wells doe drive away the Toades, with which their Wells are much infected …'

In more recent times, and with the aid of science, two eminent archaeologists, Wainwright and Darvill, proposed evidence that Stonehenge was a prehistoric hospice. They claimed the blue stones were considered to hold restorative properties, which might explain their use when the monument was first constructed. Yet where there is life, so there is death – and the diseased, sacrificed and dead are always more interesting to the 1 million visitors each year.

Even individual stones have names which evoke suffering and gore. The Slaughter Stone, now fallen into its recumbent position, is aged and pockmarked and the rain collects in the round hollows that pepper the surface. Iron within the stone turns the water blood red which those in antiquity (namely the Victorians) believed was sacrificed blood – hence its name.

Stonehenge imagined – how it might once have looked. (Courtesy of the Wiltshire and Swindon History Centre)

More gruesome still, the Altar Stone, lying at the heart of the monument, is flat and well suited to the idea of ritual killing. What horrors took place on this recumbent slab?

The Heel Stone, standing sentinel as the processional avenue enters the henge, has a companion bearing the same name. It too harbours a devilish legend. Merlin, the Arthurian magician, brought these stones from Ireland, incurring the wrath of the Devil. In a rage, the Devil threw the colossal stone which caught the wizard on the heel, the resulting indentation still visible today. A similar legend exists for the upright Heel Stone, but here Merlin is replaced by an unwitting friar who disturbs the Devil as he builds his Stonehenge.

Almost inevitably (though incorrectly), the 'mystical' druids were credited (or blamed) for constructing Stonehenge, as a temple where they could carry out their hideous customs. Aubrey and William Stukeley, both eminent antiquarians, independently concluded almost a century apart that the mysterious bards and priests were responsible for this Druidic shrine. As the priests laid their victims on the Altar Stone, their golden sickles silencing their screams, fresh blood gathered beneath the stone as the audience cried out to the gods.

Fanciful as these claims are, death and burial have indeed taken place at Stonehenge ever since it was first built. Often brutal, sometimes punishment, on occasion surely sacrifice, body after body made its final journey to this once isolated spot on Salisbury Plain. In 2600 BC, at least fifty-five cremations were interred in a circle of holes

A Victorian idea of what the druids may have looked like. (THP)

(known as the Aubrey Holes after their discoverer): loved ones, enemies, perhaps even shamans, burnt close by and placed here with reverence (or contempt).

Yet it is the skeletons that attract the most attention. One in particular was found buried outside the outer bluestone circle. Dated as an Anglo-Saxon, his head had been removed with a single blow and dropped onto his chest before his humiliatingly small grave was backfilled with soil and chalk. Decapitation in Early Medieval (Saxon) England was an established practice. But did this make him a criminal: executed for some grave misdemeanour (no pun intended!), or a sacrifice, offered to the gods? Whatever the truth, in death he was as unfortunate as he had been in life.

When first discovered, his remains were sent to London for examination by the Royal College of Surgeons where, it was believed, he fell victim again, this time to the air raids of the Luftwaffe. Forgotten for over fifty years, he was

THE BOSCOMBE BOWMEN

Were the Boscombe Bowmen – a collection of 'warrior' skeletons found near Amesbury – a peripatetic workforce from Europe who helped erect Stonehenge, or something else completely? One thing is certain: when they died in around 2300 BC, there was a gruesome oddity in the way they had been buried. For the Bowmen held special heirlooms, unlike any other, on their journey into the afterlife. These seven individuals were not all of one time – some were in fact far older, by many generations. It meant they were carrying the carefully selected bones of their ancestors; keepsakes, not of jewellery or precious metal, but body parts from their forebears.

Stonehenge now. (David J. Vaughan)

rediscovered in 1999 – down the road, at the Natural History Museum.

Finally, of the many dead associated with Stonehenge, none is perhaps more important than the Amesbury Archer, found close to the town bearing his name. This traveller from mainland Europe, probably Switzerland, had been greatly revered when he died in 2300 BC. His treasure trove of grave goods featured gold artefacts, copper daggers, tinder for starting fires, oyster shell, boars' tusks, possibly a much-prized bow with arrows (their shafts long since eroded) and the list goes on. It remains the richest grave from the period ever found and suggests this was not a warrior then, more an artisan, a leader of people, perhaps directing others during the construction of Stonehenge.

AD 552–1003

DEATH, PUNISHMENT AND WAR

Grave Days for the Saxons

ONE OF THE largest Saxon burial grounds in Wiltshire lies in Harnham, south of Salisbury. It was discovered in 1853 by Mr Wallan the 'Drowner' – he who floods the water meadows – in Low Field (named after the Anglo-Saxon *hlæw*, meaning tumulus). His keen eye recognised a spear tip, the great boss of a wooden shield and the disturbed human skeletons rising through the earth. They could only be Saxon. Within days, archaeologists found sixty-two graves – men, women and children – and not all had died peacefully in their sleep.

In any pagan Saxon cemetery, the grave goods alone speak of great violence. Here at Harnham, knives, shields and swords joined spears – with at least one designed to rotate in the air and penetrate deeper into the flesh. They evoked war and aggression, even if some were ceremonial in this context of the dead. Meanwhile, the skeletons too evoked suffering. One, a female, had been buried with her infant placed deliberately between her knees, as though life had left both in unison.

Others had been cruelly weighted down, with flint and broken pottery pressing them to the floor. It is now believed to indicate death by *felo de se* (suicide), often while the victim was considered temporarily insane, and Christian Saxons insisted that such deaths be given the old-style pagan burial, devoid of any Christian respect. There was no place in heaven for those who died by their own hand.

At Roche Court Down, north-east along the modern A30 to Lopcombe Corner, another Saxon grave contained some eighteen skeletons. Four had their wrists tied behind their backs, while half had been decapitated. Common criminals? Enemies? Not all beheadings were punishments for misdemeanours and many of the cuts here had been made to the neck by swords swung from the front, intended to stop the spirit of the dead rising to haunt the living. However, the Saxon killing and burial of a criminal was equally brutal. Pre-mortem amputation removed the hand of a thief and a prone (face down) skeleton overlying one supine (face up) indicated that either the person on the top had been sacrificed or, more likely, had been convicted of causing the death of the person placed beneath. As punishment they were buried alive with their victim.

Decapitation sanctioned by Heaven. (British Library Board, Cotton Claudius B IV f 38r)

In contexts such as the burial at Stonehenge, Saxon decapitation may have had more to do with appeasing the gods than satisfying a demand for worldly justice. The sword was swift and, as seen in this detail taken from a Saxon manuscript, it was also endorsed by Heaven.

Salisbury has not yet given up much evidence for the Early Medieval period, in particular its wars between the Saxons, Celts and Danes. We can be sure, however, that their customs and attitudes to death were enacted here just as elsewhere. In AD 552, when Cyrnic conquered Old Sarum, the number and treatment of those who died in battle could be considered barbaric. As recorded in an Anglo-Saxon chronicle, this warrior leader of the West Saxons took Searobyrg by force, dealing with those who stood in his way with savagery and little remorse. The Saxons not only bound and executed their enemies but, in many cases, they buried them alive. Ten skeletons buried in a surviving Bronze Age round barrow had their hands tied behind their backs and had been inhumed face down. Gruesome indeed: the terror of those ten is palpable. Placed inside the fresh grave, soil and chalk heaped upon their backs, their mouths ingesting the earth as they were unable to move, speak or, eventually, to breathe. How they must have willed death to come …

Three hundred years later, in the reign of King Alfred, the Danes arrived. At a raised spot in Wilton, a violent struggle erupted. Alfred, as so often, was victorious. But a century and more later, they returned, this time under Sweyn's command. By now, the Saxon leaders had no stomach for war and instead abandoned their people and fled to Old Sarum, the hill which their more lion-hearted ancestors had conquered five centuries before. Left alone, Sweyn burnt Wilton to the ground before his army made for Salisbury, pausing en route at the old hill fort. The Saxons, it seemed, would have to fight whether or not their hearts were in it.

A FASCINATION WITH THE DEAD

—◦∞◦—

Society in the medieval period – in particular, the Saxons – was obsessed with reusing existing sites of death and ritual. It was as if they sought association with the ancestors, or perhaps supernatural gains from these surviving monuments. Chief amongst their preferred locations were the round barrows of the Bronze Age. Hundreds of Saxon inhumations and cremations have been found, usually in the upper levels of these earthen mounds, often complete with elaborate grave goods. There were others though – hill forts (from the Iron Age), ditches, ringworks and rarer, but not unknown, prehistoric stone circles – surely more to do with reaching the 'other world' than securing a place in this.

—◦∞◦—

Before Saxon Salisburians turned to Christ, they occasionally constructed unusually rich, pagan graves. Artefacts placed with the body included intricately worked jewellery, pottery, metal vessels, glassware, precious stones – and the ubiquitous array of weapons. The most famous locally lies in a cemetery at nearby Collingbourne Ducis with its iconic 'treasure' the 'bed burial'. These status symbols were typically provided for adult women, whose bodies lay supported on a plank bed fixed with iron nails and gave the impression of wealth and power. But, as well as material objects, the important dead required something else to escort them on their final journey. Human sacrifices often included servants slaughtered during the funeral, or sometimes old foes, summarily executed. The Saxon attitude to life and death was indeed harsh.

The Viking visits the Celt. As imagined in 1868! (Author's collection)

AD 961–1538

MISCHIEVOUS MONKS AND WANTON NUNS

Leaving the Straight and Narrow

O what can be worse than this life that I dree,
When naughty and lovelorn and wanton I be?

Avoiding the old joke about having dirty habits, the men and women of the religious houses at Salisbury created more than their fair share of mischief and mayhem. And, although the wanton women of Wilton brought the greatest shame on their supposedly virtuous souls, we begin here with the men.

Before 1234, the grey Franciscan friars set up their house south of the present St Ann Street toward Bugmore. But by the time of Henry VIII's Dissolution of the Monasteries, these friars had been sucked into the wickedness of the world outside. In particular, they were embroiled in economic woe and bad debt. In fact, things had sunk so low that a certain Charles Bulkeley petitioned the king's chief minister, Thomas Cromwell, to be allowed to purchase the friars' house, acting before the king himself took possession. He had, he wrote, stayed in that house for twenty years, paying an annual rent of 26s 8d, which he knew was the friars' only source of income.

He offered £100 for the buildings and a further 100 marks for the jewels and plate. To no avail. When Henry ordered its closure, all the friars' goods were sold and even then it left debts unpaid. Bulkeley paid his final rent and left.

The black friars of St Dominic fared little better, after establishing their first house at Wilton in 1245. By 1281, with the town lying in social and economic ruin, they relocated to Fisherton Anger, closer to the episcopal seat of Salisbury. Notwithstanding the reputation of the Dominicans for their part in the cruel Inquisition, fighting witchcraft and paganism with a brutal terror, several of the friars soon showed more compassion than judgment when taking the law into their own hands. During the reign of Edward II, a certain John, son of William de Tynhide, had been imprisoned in Old Sarum and sentenced to death. His misdemeanours are not known but were presumably grave. On the fateful day, as he was led from the gaol to the gallows, he passed by the Dominican friary from whence five monks leapt on the bailiffs, cut the rope that bound John's hands and set the bemused man free. All were arrested but eventually given royal

Sedentes in tenebris & in Vmbra
Mortis Vinctos in mendicitate. Psal. 106

(With kind permission of the Thomas Fisher
Rare Book Library, Library of Toronto)

pardons and their motivation has never been discovered.

In the past, these Dominicans had followed their Franciscan brothers by accepting support only in kind. In Salisbury, it included timber for their church from William de Longespée but, by the fourteenth century, they soon realised this was quite impractical. Thereafter, most gifts arrived in the form of hard cash or items of great intrinsic value and, by the time of the closure of their house in 1538, they had amassed a great inventory of silver, plate and jewels. These were lost, however, when the Bishop of Dover, carrying out an assessment of compliance for Henry VIII, took from them not just their goods and chattels but the buildings themselves. The monks were forced to leave and a Dominican presence in Salisbury had reached an ignominious end.

For all their troubles with money and irate monarchs, the monks of all denominations were saints compared to the nearby nuns! The most controversial at Salisbury were the Benedictine nuns of Wilton Abbey. Founded by King Alfred in the ninth century, originally thirteen women 'took the veil', but these wild women of Wilton were never going to be the shy, retiring maids expected of such an institution.

One of the first abbesses was named Wulfhryth. In around 961 she begat King Edgar's illegitimate daughter, Edith, after she had been snatched away by the lusty monarch. Despite such 'promiscuity', she returned to Wilton with her bastard child and in time became abbess – surely not the conventional rite of passage into convent life. It was a sign of things to come.

Edith followed her mother's example in later becoming abbess and in having a strong character and delivering acerbic put-downs. When reprimanded by Saint Adelwold, the Bishop of Winchester, for wearing fancy clothes and being altogether too unseemly, the young woman replied that she in her garments of gold thread could be just as virtuous as he in his filthy skins! In fact, the propensity of the Wilton women, whether deliberate or not, for attracting powerful men was legendary.

In 1093, when King William (Rufus) visited the abbey, he immediately lusted after Matilda, daughter of Malcolm, King of Scotland and a child scholar at the convent. The abbess, knowing something of the king's reputation, disguised Matilda as a nun when Rufus came to call, accompanied by Malcolm who had recommended his daughter for

Great Seal of William Rufus, King of England (1087–1100). (George Lillie Craik et al)

a regal match. When the king veered off into the cloisters, claiming he wanted to look at the roses, he clapped eyes on the girl complete with her veil and stormed off in thwarted disgust. A week later, having been severely chastised by the frustrated king, Matilda's father returned to the abbey. Striding up to his daughter, he tore off the offending garment, stamped it underfoot and left, this time taking her with him. It is not recorded whether or not she was glad of it, but some say it was she who had so violently removed the veil.

The first misdemeanours of the institution's abbey were, like the grey friars, in the form of bad debts. In the mid-thirteenth century, the convent buildings had been allowed to fall into such decay that the Bishop of Salisbury had to divert revenues from other churches to render the necessary repairs. Even the shrine to St Edith was in danger of collapse. Some forty or so years later, they faced excommunication by the Dean of Salisbury after the abbess had fallen gravely behind in repaying a loan he had made to them back in 1281.

Against this backdrop of financial imprudence, the discipline of the women fell like a lead weight. In 1284 and again

Seals of Edith, Abbess of Wilton. (Wiltshire Archaeology and Natural History Magazine, Vol. 19)

in 1302, during separate interregnums when no abbess was appointed to maintain order, the Wilton nuns were found guilty of gross misconduct. And when they had an abbess, in 1317 she was found to be too old and infirm to fulfil her duties, particularly the moral and worldly rectitude of her charges. In fact, the women were running riot! A canon of Salisbury Cathedral was appointed to restore – and maintain – spiritual order, but these nuns were not so easily deterred!

In 1379, the bishop visited the abbey and was horrified at what he found. It was, he said, more like a women's refuge than a religious house. He demanded the immediate end to their wanton practices: to live within their means, desist from letting all and sundry enter the house, especially to stop giving access to married women seeking sanctuary and to carry out punishments of miscreant nuns in public, not in private! The bishop also ordered the nuns to stop entertaining themselves – in superstitious and pagan plays and games.

They were still having none of it. As late as 1521, their reputation plunged further as they were now sued for yet another unpaid bill, this one for 'vestments of silk and velvet wrought with gold and powdered with archangels'. Their response to the petition was blunt – they claimed to have paid for the items in wool from the abbey sheep, as arranged. What's more, the plaintiff had been provided with food and drink while he collected it! One wonders, however, if food, drink and wool were the only means of payment ...

Seven years later came perhaps their darkest hour. Anne Boleyn, second wife of Henry VIII, became embroiled in the election of a new abbess which saw Henry caught between his troublesome queen and the church. The mudslinging that ensued was both bitter and damaging. Anne supported Eleanor Carey, long-time inhabitant of the abbey and sister of the queen's brother-in-law, William Carey. However, Anne's rival, Cardinal Wolsey, wanted another of the nuns, Isabel Jordayne. Well aware of the abbey's reputation, he considered her to be 'ancient, wise – and discreet'! To ensure success, he had Eleanor's past investigated and what colourful reading it made. Mother to two bastard children, each by a serving priest, she had recently

Henry VIII, who publically chastised Cardinal Wolsey. (THP)

been engaged in a relationship with an unnamed servant!

It left Anne incandescent. Convincing Henry that Isabel was no angel either, the king was forced to object to her appointment because she 'either be or have been at any time noted or spotted with incontinence, like as by report the prioress had been in her youth'. When Wolsey went ahead and appointed Isabel anyway, Henry secretly agreed but, fearful of upsetting his queen, he publicly chastised the senior cleric. Wilton Abbey, it seemed, would always have its unruly reputation and by the time of the Dissolution, it had long fallen into ruin.

AD 1092

THE BISHOP IS IN THE COWSHED!

King v. Church in Old Salisbury

OLD SARUM BEGAN medieval life as the king's bastille. William I ('the Conqueror') held court there in 1086, when 60,000 of his new principal subjects were ordered to swear fealty to their new monarch and to accept Domesday, the national account of possessions across his kingdom. Nonetheless, eyebrows were raised when Old Sarum was selected for Bishop Herman's new cathedral. The former Iron Age hill fort was regarded as most unsuitable and for two very good reasons: (i) it was a castle and a fortified 'state', not a true town and (ii) it meant the clergy would live cheek by jowl with the king's men, namely his soldiers – 'the Ark of God shut up in the Temple of Baal'. It therefore came as no surprise to many when, just five days after Bishop Osmund (Bishop Herman's successor) consecrated the new edifice in 1092, God's new house on the hill was destroyed by a thunderstorm that tore off the tower roof and flattened much of the walling. It seemed that even the Almighty disapproved of his bishop's choice.

Bishop Osmund was William I's nephew. Nevertheless, before long, cracks in the family ties (like those in the new cathedral) began to appear. William II (William Rufus), the Conqueror's son and Osmund's cousin, was not as liberal as his father – in fact, Rufus proved himself to be utterly ruthless. Beyond the walls of Old Sarum, he fell out with Anselm, Archbishop of Canterbury, by insisting with force that the investiture of new bishops was only the king's right to perform, a standpoint that set him at loggerheads with his kinsman bishop.

After Osmund died in 1099, the merciless Rufus took charge of Old Sarum Cathedral but a year later, was mysteriously felled by a 'stray' arrow as he rode through the New Forest. His successor, Henry I, then appointed Roger of Avranches as the new bishop, chiefly for the speed with which he got through the often tedious Mass! He rewarded him with control of the castle and once more the line between king and bishop grew blurred. So close was he

William I, 'the Conqueror', who held court at Old Sarum. (THP)

Percutiam Paſtorem, & diſpergen-
tur ouos gregus. *Matt. 26. Mar. 14.*

*(With kind permission of the Thomas Fisher
Rare Book Library, Library of Toronto)*

now to Henry that people referred to him as *secundus a Rege* (second after the king). Indeed, as his self-styled justiciar, he made himself responsible for the king's finances, often using eye-wateringly brutal methods (*see* text box). As so often with such abusers of power, scurrilous and damaging rumours soon circulated. The unmarried Roger had taken a concubine, producing at least one child who the hypocritical bishop passed off as his nephew. As his unpopularity grew, he removed himself further from his church and turned instead to building castles. One of his finest was at Devizes where he installed his 'nephew' as castellan. Now the cleric was becoming a threat to the Crown.

Following King Henry's death in 1135, things unravelled spectacularly for the unholy prelate. The Anarchy Wars from that year saw great quantities of vitriol, pride and bloodshed as the family squabble reached all-out war. Roger characteristically hunted with the hounds and ran with the hare until King Stephen, growing tired of his unfaithful bishop, had him arrested at the Great Council at Oxford in 1139 after a fatal, some say engineered, mêlée involving his heavily armed entourage. Having embattled knights not only broke ecclesiastical law, it sent a message of defiance to the king! The affronted Stephen immediately detained the once mighty Roger, and had him imprisoned – in a cowshed! Moreover, he seized his castles which, in the case of Devizes, came only after threatening to hang his son if the bishop or his 'nephew' resisted. Now without property, previously symbolic of his worldly if not spiritual might, Roger was eventually returned to Old Sarum if not a prisoner then a spent force. He died a few weeks later, bitter and broken and deeply resented.

Like him, the church had never been so unpopular. At Old Sarum, a century later, the king's garrison and the clergy repeatedly confronted one another as violence erupted. Soldier and canon allegedly exchanged '[b]rawls and sadde blowes'; while disputes over rights of entry to the castle 'ended in violence and abuse'. Moreover, the king's men increasingly prevented pilgrims from entering the cathedral precinct, claiming they breached security. The final straw

*King Stephen, who locked
Roger in a cowshed. (THP)*

BISHOP ROGER'S CASTRATED COINERS

Medieval punishments were harsh, none more so than for coining – counterfeiting the king's money. And it was down to our old friend, Bishop Roger, as treasurer to Henry I, to dispense justice – Anglo-Saxon style.

Following complaints by the king's knights that their pay contained more tin than silver, the guilty coiners were arrested and, at Christmas 1125, placed before Roger to face their doom. Despite passionately pleading their innocence, each man was castrated, blinded and, on the orders of the king, removed of his right hand.

This reintroduced a Saxon penalty where either the eyes, the appendage or both were nailed to the door of the victim's house to serve as a warning to others!

Old Sarum Castle. (Courtesy of the Wiltshire and Swindon History Centre)

their faces, a provocative act that could not go unpunished. The incumbent bishop, Richard Poore, reportedly exclaimed to his canons:

> When they persecute you in one city, flee ye into another … I vow and promise to Almighty God and the Blessed Virgin Mary, that, life being granted to me, I will labour earnestly to build an abode and a church for the chaste Virgin, the Mother of Christ, away from the King's Castle, and removed from the royal power; and you, my children, bear ye your burden yet a little while for verily the days are evil.

came after 1217, when the canons, returning from their Rogationtide procession, drew near to the castle gates. As they approached, members of the garrison swung the castle gates shut in

After years of hostility and bad blood, that new abode became the magnificent cathedral church of the Blessed Virgin Mary which, together with its Close, formed a New Salisbury. Yet soon that too attracted blood and most ungodly behavior.

AD 1096

THE DEFEAT AND MUTILATION OF WILLIAM D'EU

Trial by Combat

WHEN A PAIR of iron shackles were discovered at Old Sarum, still attached to the legs of a skeleton buried to the north-east of the cathedral choir, the hunt was on to identify who had been found. The deduction, controversial but plausible, was William d'Eu, Early Medieval baron and cousin of William the Conqueror. This can hardly be confirmed, of course, but if it is him, he must have truly annoyed his captors. The body also had no head.

William d'Eu (aka Guillaume Comte d'Eu) was one of the original Anglo-Norman barons installed by the king following his conquest of 1066. In the end, though, d'Eu proved himself a traitor and not just once. On the first occasion, in 1087, he joined a rebellion against his own kinsman, King William I.

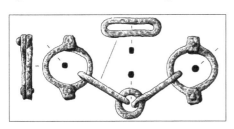

The iron shackles found on d'Eu's skeleton. (With kind permission of the Salisbury and South Wiltshire Museum)

Though the coup failed, the king forgave d'Eu and soon after visited the lucky earl at his manor in Lacock where all seemed well, all troubles forgotten.

But cometh the king's successor, cometh a new rebellion. William Rufus (aka William II, the Conqueror's son) was not so forgiving. Accounts written long after the events tell us quite clearly how William d'Eu was again indicted for his involvement in a baronial dispute, this time Robert de Mowbray's failed rebellion of 1095. More sinisterly, this one included a plot to murder the new king and to put his cousin, Stephen of Aumale, on the throne in his place. Intercepting four Norwegian ships and refusing Rufus' demands for the return of the cargo, the conspirators were arrested and subsequently tried at Old Sarum castle.

While the others suffered less extreme or, at least, less protracted punishments – even Mowbray himself was only imprisoned – William d'Eu suffered more than most. His accuser, Geoffrey Baynard, had been High Sheriff of York, a crucial position for it carried access to the king's ear. Whether or not he could believe one of his most noble barons to be false, Rufus avoided passing judgment and instead

LEGAL TRIAL, NORMAN STYLE

Trial by combat (in England usually 'wager of battle') was mostly fought between nobles caught up in a personal dispute, often over land. Clad in full armour, each party would be expected to fight armed with longsword, dagger and spear though, in truth, they made use of almost anything they could lay their hands on. Fighting was not necessarily to the death; a panel of up to three judges were empowered to call an end to the trial if they thought one party had been truly overwhelmed by the other.

Under Henry II, it was frequently replaced with a 'trial by ordeal'. Here, the unfortunate accused could undergo various forms of torture to determine their guilt in the eyes of God. For male serfs, this usually meant trial by water but for everyone else, women included, it was trial by hot irons.

Trial by combat remained a legal form of 'justice' until 1819 and the last recorded challenge occurred just two years earlier. Abraham Thornton, acquitted of the murder of Mary Ashton, was rearrested following an appeal by the dead woman's brother. Thornton shocked the court by demanding trial by battle, a petition they felt forced to grant. But it was never carried into effect. Soon after, the law was changed, so hastily that all three required readings of the Bill were passed in the House of Lords in one night!

ordered Baynard and d'Eu to fight out their differences in a trial by combat.

This gruesome mode of 'justice' was hugely popular in the early Medieval period and remained so until the mid-fifteenth century. And William, like Geoffrey, knew it was less important to win than not to lose. For victory meant little more than saving face, but to be defeated meant a punishment of hideous brutality. To the victor the spoils; to the loser, blinding and castration!

The trial took place at Old Sarum in January 1096 and William lost. With horror in his heart, he was placed in iron shackles and kept in the castle to await his cruel fate. Soon enough, it was mercilessly dispensed. Never recovering from his torture, William died soon after and so began the mystery of what happened next. Some say he was buried not in Salisbury but at his home in Hastings, near the site of his relation's famous victory over Harold thirty years before. Others maintain he was buried where he fell. And, if they are correct, the skeleton in the leg irons found at Old Sarum is all the more likely to be the late, rebellious baron.

Footnote: Whoever the skeleton truly is, he has dramatically dismissed the long-held belief amongst historians that iron shackles such as these were only used on wayward animals. They differ from the normal chain-linked ankle cuffs, having instead a rigid bar, not padlocked or secured with a key but riveted, and are impossible to remove without further violence against the wearer. Once they were fitted, the poor man at Old Sarum would have been unable to take steps of more than 6in (14cm), making his escape improbable.

AD 1219

SPIRES OF DOOM!

Salisbury's Unholy Past

IT IS STRANGELY fitting that the move of the cathedral from Old Sarum to what is now Salisbury, and the development of its associated Close, began with the consecration of a cemetery at Myrifield (Mary-field). As the new edifice rose up towards Heaven, many thought it would bring an age of peace, forgiveness and salvation. Instead, in the eight centuries since its foundation stones were laid, it has witnessed an attempted murder, mayhem, war and so much death.

It is hard to imagine that the construction alone of such a colossus of Early English architecture could not have witnessed its fair share of accidents and fatalities, especially as the structure grew higher and more perilous and the

An old engraving showing Salisbury Cathedral with its former bell tower. (Author's collection)

walls began to splay under the weight of the new tower.

As soon as it was built, the first official act was the translation of the remains of three long-dead bishops from Old Sarum – Osmund, Roger and Jocelin – so that the new dawn had begun with the old dead. It would prove an omen.

In 1448, a servant of one of the residential canons was beaten to death following some so-called tomfoolery by young choristers. Armed with sticks and batons, the older man succumbed to their uncontrollable mischief as ill-discipline rode roughshod over saintly decorum. Singers had been employed by non-residential canons to stand in during the often long and tedious services, but, unfortunately, ribald songs were not their only boisterous pleasure ...

The cathedral, having survived the medieval visitation of the plague and the danger of changing attitudes toward religion, suffered a spectacular fall from grace. Initially, it endured theft and ransacking and, in the space of forty-seven years from 1536, its holy treasures of three large silver-gilt chalices and patens, eight smaller chalices and plenty more were removed by person or persons

Salisbury Cathedral. (LC-DIG-ppmsc-08826)

unknown so that by 1583 it was left with just twenty-nine artefacts 'of little value'. Toward the end of that period, an attempted murder of one of its deans shook the already reeling house of God to its foundations.

The attacker – one John Farrant – was cathedral choir master and its chief organist. For some inexplicable reason, he left midway through a service to cross the Close to the deanery (now the Old Deanery) where he knew the dean would be sitting in his study, working on church business. As he entered the room, the startled dean jumped to his feet and Farrant made to stab him in the chest. He was using a knife which he had either brought secreted beneath his robes or had collected on his way through the dean's house. The frightened man escaped by racing upstairs and locking himself in his bedroom, thwarting his would-be assassin until he eventually left. Incredibly, Farrant then returned to the cathedral where he resumed his seat

in the choir and finished taking part in the service!

Unsurprisingly, a hearing was held the next day but Farrant failed to attend and soon after disappeared from the diocese. The reasons behind his irrational behaviour went with him, but we find him a year later as organist and choir master at Hereford Cathedral. Here, he was listed similarly as one of those chastised for vile and inappropriate conduct!

Between 1642 and 1659, England fought to be a republic and a new religious intolerance led to the cathedral entering an interregnum, when no bishop was appointed and no universal authority allowed. Indeed, it became more secular than sacred. It was Salisbury's lowest ebb: the Close was used as a rubbish dump, butchers killed and sold their meats there and coaches used the churchyard as a shortcut, churning up the ground and smashing the graves. At the same time, the cloisters, far from being a place of quiet contemplation, were used to house Dutch prisoners of war and suffered irreparable damage. The dream of the bishops of Old Sarum had descended into Gomorrah.

The cloisters where Dutch prisoners of war were held. (Author's collection)

The remaining tale in this abridged chapter reads more like a trumped-up ghost story than a real moment in Salisbury's tragic history. Credit here is due to Peter Underwood.

There was an old stately hall which once stood in the shadow of the great cathedral spire. It had as much antiquity as it had charm and, in one of its many panelled rooms, a section of the floor was worn down more than anywhere else. It was as if it had known frequent to-ings and fro-ings, such as would be found near a door. One evening a house guest was urged to inspect the mysteriously smoothed patch which that night reflected the meagre candlelight with an unnatural intensity. At first, the investigator could find nothing unusual and, partly in frustration, stamped his foot on the worn boards. To his astonishment, a section of the oak panelling instantly swung open and revealed a hidden cupboard, complete with shelf. Running his hand around its walls he found he could ease the shelf sideways and saw, hidden behind, a small door.

Agreeing with his host to carry on, he pushed it open to discover a stone spiral staircase that ascended within the chimney breast, reaching so high that it quite disappeared from view. As they climbed, their hearts beating, they reached a small platform set out just below the joists. It was just big enough to allow someone to sit or lie and the two men squeezed themselves forward with some difficulty. It was soon apparent that they had found a secret observatory, not for monitoring the stars but for spying on the neighbours – utilising a clear gap in the gaping mouth of the gargoyle on the wall outside.

Dismissing this contrivance for what it was, the men were about to leave when a hand touched something smooth – a ragged but now disintegrating scrap of velvet – and there was something beneath. Lifting it clear, he revealed a desiccated yet perfectly articulated human skeleton, its hand still grasping a letter and a small ring. Now the men were intent on finding out more about the real-life skeleton in the closet.

It took time to interpret the evidence – for that was the title it merited – and eventually, after extensive research, an explanation as sad as any was unearthed. In time immemorial, a young Salisbury doctor had purchased the hall for his intended and much-beloved wife. The night before their wedding, tragedy struck as the bride-to-be fell gravely ill and very soon after breathed her last.

The doctor was so struck with grief that his friends grew afraid of his morose nature and they tried desperately to tease him away from the city for a holiday and a change of air, to put some distance between himself and his tragic loss. However, the medic insisted on remaining alone and was allowed to grieve in peace. A number of weeks later, when no one had seen him leave the house, his neighbours broke into the hall deeply afraid of what they might find. But, in fact, they found nothing. The doctor, it seemed, had gone on that holiday after all.

The poor man was never seen or heard of again; until the visitor to his house discovered the hidden attic and the stairs at the back of the cupboard. Grief can affect us in many deep and heartfelt ways.

AD 1226

THE WARLORD, THE SKULL AND THE RAT

An 800-Year-Old Murder Mystery

IN SALISBURY CATHEDRAL lies the tomb of William Longespée, thirteenth-century nobleman, king's warlord, royal bastard and the first person to be buried in the cathedral in 1226. How William ended up in his elaborate tomb – and what happened when curious antiquaries opened it up several hundred years later – has produced a medieval tale of power, hypocrisy and cowardly murder.

William Longespée, nicknamed Longsword because of his giant stature (though possibly also for the size of his fabled weapon!), was the illegitimate son of King Henry II. His half-brother became King Richard I, who promptly married him off to Ela, Amesbury-born daughter of the 2nd Earl of Salisbury. She was just 9 years of age and would become central to her husband's premature and mysterious death.

Longespée, it seemed, could make enemies easily. His continued allegiance to King John cast him in the role of villain to the rebellious barons, before he eventually jumped ship. As a statement of acquiescence to England's disgruntled nobility, he began persuading the unpopular monarch to sign Magna Carta (of which one of only

thirteen original copies is kept in the library at Salisbury Cathedral). William's inconsistency and sedition, rather than securing support and popularity, put his life in mortal danger from all sides; especially from another signatory at Runnymede, Hubert de Burgh.

Writing some years later, Roger of Wendover accused Hubert (a distant ancestor of the singer, Chris de Burgh) of poisoning William after the latter sided with King Louis of France following the death of King John. Hubert had ordered William to support John's son, Henry, who was William's nephew (illegitimate), but William refused. Heads finally collided when William led a party of Louis' agents to Hubert's castle, urging the latter to relinquish to the new French 'king'.

The meeting at the castle postern was difficult. William arrived with Thomas, Hubert's brother, who had initially been taken captive during Louis' assault on Norwich. Hubert though, brought five retainers, all holding a crossbow, fully charged and ready to unleash hell upon the 'traitors'.

William spoke first. He promised that if Louis was forced to take possession of the castle by force – and take it he would – those within its walls would be hanged. Thomas spoke next through his tears, imploring his brother to have compassion on those gathered here, to free them all from certain death.

Then William spoke a soliloquy:

> Listen to my advice, Hubert, and obey the will of our lord Louis, and he will give you, as an inheritance, the counties of Norfolk and Suffolk ... but, if you do not, your brother Thomas will be hung, and you in a short time will suffer the same.

Some choice!

Hubert responded with hatred:

> Earl, wicked traitor that you are, although king John ... your brother be dead, he has heirs, namely your nephew, whom, although every body else deserted him, you, his uncle, ought not to abandon ... why then, base and wicked man that you are, do you talk thus to me. Do not speak another word, because ... if you open your mouth to say any thing more, you shall all be pierced with numbers of arrows, nor will I spare my own brother.

Seeing that the disgruntled Hubert meant business, William and Thomas beat their hasty retreat.

The relationship between William and Hubert soured further. Returning from his latest sea voyage, William accused his nemesis of abusing his wife Ela and attempting to take her as his own. He made his claim in front of the young king, by now Henry III, and Hubert knew he would suffer if the allegations were ever proved. Instantly and prudently, he

William Longespée: the illustration based on his tomb. (Author's collection)

apologised, inviting William to 'share his table' that night.

William accepted, a decision he would soon regret. That evening, he ate and drank from his host's larder, then rose suddenly, apologised to Hubert and announced that he must leave. He withdrew to Salisbury Castle feeling gravely ill and was dead within hours. William Longespée had succumbed to a mysterious illness.

His funeral was attended by a who's who of medieval nobility with King Henry himself as chief mourner. William was laid to rest first in the Lady Chapel but later, by around 1240, in his tomb of decorated oak and gilded Doulting stone placed in the nave. His was the first burial inside the new cathedral and his effigy still attracts visitors each year. Rumours surrounding his death focused on his last supper with Hubert and in 1791, antiquarians finally broke into his tomb and were confronted with a truly gruesome find. Inside the earl's otherwise empty skull were the mortal remains of a rat (now on display at the Salisbury and South Wiltshire Museum). No doubt trapped after enjoying an opportunist's meal of flesh and human brains, its pathetic corpse was removed and tested by experts aware of the poisoning rumours. To their horror and delight, a quantity of arsenic was found in its rotting carcass. Roger of Wendover, it seemed, had been right all along.

AD 1483

BUCKINGHAM LOSES HIS HEAD!

Be Careful What You Wish For

O, in the battle think on Buckingham,
And die in terror of thy guiltiness!
Dream on, dream on, of bloody deeds
and death:
Fainting, despair; despairing, yield thy
breath!

Ghost of Buckingham to Richard III
(*Richard III*, Shakespeare)

Eagle-eyed visitors to Salisbury will have
spied a blue plaque on a wall around the
corner from Debenhams. Written upon
it is the simple inscription:

It was here that Henry, Duke of
Buckingham was executed on Sunday
November 2nd 1483 in the reign of
Richard III.

Buckingham played a central role in
the turbulent and bloody history of
England's War of the Roses and was
forever immortalised in Shakespeare's
play, *Richard III*. His death in Salisbury
was no accident.

In 1483, the city lay at the heart of
a western insurgency that epitomised
a violent struggle between Yorkist King
Richard III and Lancastrian supporters
of Henry Tudor. It was a bloody time

and nowhere escaped its carnage and
brutality. A key moment in the future of
the English monarchy was soon being
acted out in the city of Salisbury and the
open yards of its hostelries.

By the time the hunchback king
entered through the city gates, his
single intention was to put down the
uprising which Buckingham, his former
ally, had attempted to raise. The pair
had fallen out spectacularly, perhaps
over their rumoured involvement with
the disappearance of the Princes in

Richard III. (THP)

Richard the 3ᵗʰ King of Englād
and France, Lord of Ireland

*(With kind permission of the Thomas Fisher
Rare Book Library, Library of Toronto)*

claimant, crowned King of England. In haste, he led a ragged army to the River Severn.

However, being late October, a savage storm had caused the river to burst its banks, making further passage impossible. Nature, mixed now with a dispirited and deserting militia, left Henry alone with only his generals beside him. Worse was yet to come. King Richard had heard of his old friend's intentions and was making haste to Salisbury, to wait within the castle and quash any threat to his supremacy. Buckingham's generals, learning of the king's new intelligence, abandoned Henry to his fate and fled, ironically, to the same strategically important Wiltshire city which, by good fortune, they reached first. Hearing of Richard's imminent arrival, they left again for the south coast and safe passage to Brittany. For now, there would be no bloodshed, though it was not long before the irate and embattled king entered Salisbury and declared he wanted Stafford's head on a spike.

the Tower, or perhaps from Richard's broken promise of more land for the duke.

Whatever the truth, within months of Richard's coronation, Buckingham had left court and absconded to Brecon in west Wales. Here he garnered the reluctant support of his Welsh tenants and many disgruntled nobles, all keen to see Henry Tudor, the exiled Welsh

Henry was arrested at Wem in Shropshire. Adopting threadbare clothes and the disguise of a serving man, his 'friend' Ralph Banastre, sold him down the river, taking some of Buckingham's lands as reward for 'his scalp'. Fearing for his life, he reached Salisbury on

HUMBLE ENDINGS

It is fitting that Henry Stafford and Richard III should both be recovered from such humble resting places. For Richard, too, was rediscovered ignominiously buried beneath a Leicestershire car park! Oh how far the mighty fall.

Buckingham's grave. (Courtesy of the Wiltshire and Swindon History Centre)

1 November 1483 in the company of two of Richard's knights. Immediately, he sought a meeting with the king, concealing a knife within the sleeve of his tunic and intending to cut his throat. Whether aware of his murderous intentions or just severely hacked off, Richard refused his request and simply ordered his execution without trial.

On Sunday, 2 November, All Souls' Day and despite being the Sabbath, Buckingham was led out to a spot near the Blue Boar Inn. Still wearing a shabby, pilled black cloak, he was made to kneel. His head was held firm against a block of cold stone as the axe fell. Henry Stafford, 2nd Duke of Buckingham, lay decapitated and very dead – one of England's most important rebels had met his grisly end.

Many thought this was the end of the saga but controversy rose again some centuries later. A headless skeleton with its right arm missing was discovered beneath the floor of an outhouse in the yard of the Blue Boar Inn. Despite the claims of Salisbury's great historian, Henry Hatcher, that these were indisputably the remains of the duke, others professed that his mutilated body had been interred in the church of the Grey Friars south of what is now St Ann Street. A manuscript in the Society of Antiquaries attests to this. Whatever the truth behind Stafford's final resting place, one question lies eternally unanswered – what happened to the Duke of Buckingham's head? Further claims suggest his head and missing right arm were sent to London and, as was then the custom, gruesomely displayed upon Temple Bar.

AD 1556

WHEN MEN FALL OUT, BLOOD WILL SPILL

A Right Ignoble Death

THE MOTIVATION AND causes behind the terrible events that follow have long been disputed, but the outcome and deaths it wrought are beyond doubt. Salisbury was yet again witness to the spilling of blood and a hanging in its Market Place ...

Charles, 8th Lord of Stourton, inherited a family feud that had raged between his father William and their former steward, William Hartgill of Kilmington. Circumstances reached boiling point when Stourton Sr died, for his new widow soon sought to marry her lover, a move her ill-tempered son resented. He immediately tried to block the union, offering her money from his inheritance and seeking Hartgill's help as a friend to the widowed bride. But the man refused, no doubt believing the woman old enough to make up her own mind. The quarrel that ensued outside Hartgill's home turned violent and the two men parted on unsavoury terms.

Such disputes often harbour more in their making than the final provocation but, on the following Sunday (Whitsun of that year), a brooding Charles set off with a huge party of servants for Kilmington church, intent on making Hartgill see sense. John Hartgill,

(Wiltshire Archaeology and Natural History Magazine, *Vol. 8*)

William's son, was the first to see the approaching crowd and raced to his father's house, arming himself with a longbow, crossbow and a gun, while William and his wife sought safe haven in the church tower.

Charles, though a peer of the realm, was a man of little integrity. After finding their quarry out of reach, he and his men waited for John to leave, instructed by his father to seek help from

THE STAR CHAMBER

The Star Chamber was a self-officiated court set up by the privy or other councillors and attended by the monarch. It had no jury and no witnesses and heard cases that involved the mightiest in the land, including peers of the realm. Local courts were often too afraid to try such influential people, especially if the appellant came from a so-called lower social order. The Chamber sat for over 150 years, until 1642 when it was finally abolished following abuses of power.

the highest authority. With both families being nobles, they were entitled to have their grievances heard by the queen's own council in London. As soon as John had left, Stourton returned to the church and remained for three days and nights, effectively holding William prisoner inside the tower. On the Wednesday, though, John arrived back with the High Sheriff of Somerset, causing Stourton to flee the scene, only to be arrested days later and incarcerated in Fleet prison, the gaol for felons being investigated by the Queen's Council.

On his eventual release, Stourton instigated a calendar of renewed threats

The Fleet prison pictured just before it closed. (Rudolph Ackermann)

PRESSED TO DEATH

Used in criminal trials against those who refused to enter a plea, being pressed to death (*peine forte et dure*) was law until 1772. The accused was tied spreadeagled, usually in a darkened room, and had increasingly heavy weights placed upon their chest until either they relented or simply died. Perversely, there were benefits to holding out for the latter as their heirs would then retain the right to inherit their lands whereas, if tried, found guilty and hanged, that right was forfeit. An accused's right to silence (and a presumption of innocent until proven guilty) was not introduced in England until 1827.

Being pressed to death. (Author's collection)

and 'punishments' on the Hartgill family, stealing their land and cattle and depriving William and his family of both their income and peace of mind. Only a petition to the monarch, Queen Mary, would improve the situation now and soon enough both parties were summoned before her council. Stourton was ordered once again to desist his vexatious behaviour and to recompense Hartgill for all losses. These were demands which Charles had to agree to, but only if Hartgill called on him personally to receive his dues.

It was, of course, a trick. As William and John, together with a witness, approached the house, Stourton's men emerged from the bushes and separated the younger man from the rest of the party. They set about him with ferocious force and left him for dead; which, in hindsight, was an oversight.

For John's subsequent evidence led the Queen's Council to convene a Star Chamber, (*see* text box), at which the queen herself sat. The outcome saw Stourton returned to Fleet prison with a £2,000 'bail' and £368 fine.

Before Christmas 1556, the newly liberated Charles sent a message to the Hartgills that he wished to deliver every penny of what he owed, if they would again agree to meet. Sensing further deception, William suggested the church at Kilmington for the Monday following Twelfth Night and Stourton agreed. When he arrived, though, accompanied by some sixty retainers, he suggested they move the meeting to the church house, claiming the holy church was no place for such worldly matters. Hartgill refused but, in the end, agreed to meet on the green outside. Someone procured a table for the conference.

Stourton set down a small holdall and a purse, stating by these payments, he was shown as a 'true man'. Yet it was a password. Seizing hold of the Hartgills, Stourton's henchmen dragged them into the church house as Charles declared: 'I arrest you on a charge of felony!' William and John were bound by the hands with webbing that Stourton had brought and, over several hours, their own purses and belongings were taken by Stourton and his men.

After a while, Stourton began meting out his own form of justice. He attacked first John Hartgill who, while still tied, could not defend himself. Then he turned his vindictive attentions onto the young man's wife, as she unwittingly entered the building at exactly the wrong time. In a fury, Stourton kicked the girl, using his boot-spurs to slice through her hose and injuring her legs. He then slashed her neck with the blade of his sword and left her dead in the doorway.

Stourton ordered his men to remove the two Hartgills to another of his properties, at nearby Bonham; where he continued to keep them tied, starved and thirsty. And then came Stourton's most audacious display of arrogance. He sent word to the Justices of the Peace (JP) that he had arrested the Hartgills as two felons and intended to deliver them to the gaol tomorrow. Could they come and testify to their intentions? The JPs duly arrived and agreed warrants for their trial; though they insisted that the prisoners be untied before they departed.

With the law now on his side, Stourton felt invincible. As soon as the officials had gone, he had the two men retied and within the hour had them taken outside to a close near his house. As they stood awaiting their fate, remaining silent on pain of death, two heavy wooden clubs were used to rain down blows on their unprotected heads. They fell to their knees, toppling forward as Stourton, watching from the shadows, smiled with satisfaction.

Believing them dead, both men were wrapped in their own cloaks and carried toward an outbuilding on the estate. As they were being conveyed, William Hartgill started moaning and the startled procession stopped. 'By God's blood,' one of them cried, 'they are not yet dead!'

Stourton was terrified the commotion would be heard and quickly ordered their throats to be cut. He held up a candle so his man could see where to draw the blade.

The two corpses were dropped into the dungeon beneath the outbuilding and one of Stourton's men was lowered down by rope to bury the evidence. Having dug them two graves, he dropped the corpses inside and recovered each one with earth, a pair of stone slabs and a huge quantity of timber chippings. Surely the bodies could never be found here. Stourton stood at the top, calling down to his man to hurry.

But it was not enough. For reasons not recorded, but doubtless informed by the well-known feud between the two families, Charles, 8th Earl of Stourton, was arraigned at Westminster Hall on 28 February 1557 on two charges of murder. At first, he refused to plead, relenting only when threatened with

STOURTON'S TOMB

For a man who died by the cord, it is somewhat surprising to find Charles Stourton buried in Salisbury Cathedral. His tomb, relocated to its present position, was said to have had the 'silken cord' by which he died suspended above it – replaced later by a wire in the shape of a noose. It was only taken down over 200 years later.

A more troublesome rumour is that his tomb re-used Bishop Osmund's shrine, desecrated after the Reformation. Why it should hold the body of a murderer is unclear.

being pressed to death (*see* text box). He was found guilty and sentenced to hang. His servants, too, were to be hanged, this time in chains near Kilmington. Stourton was brought back to Salisbury with his arms pinioned and his legs tied beneath his horse. On 6 March, he was hanged in the Market Place and, as a concession to his noble birth, a 'silken cord' was tied around his neck, rather than the usual rough rope. Yet it remained the ultimate insult. For nobles convicted of a capital offence, even treason, were entitled to be beheaded – hanging was for a common criminal.

Queen Mary, with her deep knowledge of Stourton's case, refused him that privilege.

A trial in action at Westminster Hall (in this case, the Georgian arraignment of the bigamous Duchess of Kingston). (THP)

AD 1627

DEATH FROM UNNATURAL CAUSES

Plague, Famine and Pestilence

TWO MEN FROM the council raised a still-breathing infant from its cot and took it away to be buried. The bubonic plague had reached Salisbury ...

In 1627, the city felt the full force of the terrible disease. Its previous dalliances with the lingering, puss-filled harbinger of death (there had been three smaller outbreaks in 1477, 1579 and 1607) had put the elders on high alert

– too high perhaps for the unfortunate babe. Burying the living in their haste to control the outbreak was not all though, as Salisbury took other strident measures.

Plague seekers, examiners and buriers of the dead were appointed and whole families were placed under curfew inside their own homes. Many more were forcibly removed to the pest-house, hastily established at Bugmore, often

The plague hits Salisbury. (THP)

taken on no more than a whim or an unsubstantiated claim from a panicky neighbour. Violence and looting erupted in the city, like pustules on infected flesh.

Everywhere was on high alert. Human barriers were set up prohibiting travellers from entering the city; public gatherings were banned; local carriers running regular services were told to stop; and all contact with London, the source of the disease, was forbidden. Salisbury's inhabitants were prisoners in their own town and many began taking their own steps to avoid the contagion. Nosegays of aromatic herbs and spices were carried, and in the cathedral and local churches, where sufferers were frequently given succour when no one else would go near them, Frankincense, rosemary and bay were strewn about the nave in an attempt to ward off the disease.

Perhaps most disturbing of all was the way in which everyone immediately fell under suspicion of being a carrier. Even the dead were suspected. New graveyards were hurriedly dug in Cathedral Green, not only to cope with the increase in casualties, but to avoid moving old corpses which people now feared might carry the invisible killer.

Mass graves and plague pits

No firm evidence of plague pits has ever been found in Salisbury, but two shallow mass graves at Old Sarum, its home before the thirteenth century, were unearthed 700 years later in 1960. Bodies buried without ceremony were shrouded in cerecloth, gathered and tied at the head and feet, while others had been tossed in haphazardly, so that many were stacked grotesquely with their limbs entwined. Was this the spot where the people of New Salisbury disposed of their infected and rotting dead, at the place they had abandoned so many years before?

Deserted medieval villages

During the horror years of the plague, many settlements around Salisbury were hit hard and populations fell like a stone. In the city itself, 6,000 or more citizens were reduced to half that number – 3,000 people struck down or escaped to the hinterland, many to die there anyway. In the worst cases, entire villages were abandoned, left to absorb the death and decay of the disease so that only the church was left standing as a morbid epitaph to the visitation of that dark evil. At Steeple Langford, north-west of the city – and as the crow flies over Old Sarum – Ballington Manor once stood south-east of where the modern A303 and A36 roads now meet. How many motorists passing this macabre spot today know how close they are to the bubonic plague? For here, homes had been built since the twelfth century and there had once been a sixteenth-century grange. All traces of that society are now gone and the only things that remain are simple earthworks in open fields.

Smallpox

For those who had survived the plague, death came once again, this time in the form of smallpox. The fatal illness, now known to have existed in the world since 10,000 BC, was especially prevalent between the eighteenth and twentieth centuries. A staggering 300 million and more people around the world died.

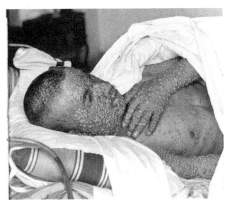

A modern case of smallpox, showing the damage to the victim's skin in lurid detail. (LC-DIG-matpc-00822)

The most obvious symptoms were the horrific eruptions on the skin and blindness, from ulceration of the cornea. It was highly infectious and yet again, poor old Bugmore housed the sick and the dying. An old house and land were acquired by Lord Folkestone in 1763 and endowed as a hospital following two terrifying outbreaks in 1723 and 1752. It was furnished through public subscription, driven by a dread of catching the disease. Efforts to inoculate had developed as far back as 1722, but in Salisbury its use had met with resistance – fearful that injecting even a small dose into the arm would spread the disease. Instead, a new infirmary was built on Fisherton Street to the north, opening in 1767, a year after the last smallpox outbreak. All was not well though; such were the conditions of the new establishment, and so virulent was the pox, that it was forced to close temporarily in 1790 and control a new epidemic which exploded within its own walls.

Leprosy

If surviving the plague and smallpox were not challenge enough for the good folk of Salisbury, other diseases and epidemics brought further misery. These included the ulcerating and disfiguring leprosy.

Old Sarum was again chosen to conceal citizens and travellers riddled with the disease. St John's Leper Hospice, dating from the twelfth century, lay to the east, although its actual location is still a matter of dispute. The renowned antiquarian, John Leland, believed it had stood in the eastern suburb just off the old hill fort but, in 2002, strong archaeological evidence was unearthed much further away. It included numerous graves – always a good sign – and a chapel, with many of the graves placed inside concentric (successive) enclosing ditches, suggesting the cemetery had been enlarged more than once. It had taken some time to bring the killer disease under control.

A second lazar house (beautifully defined in the dictionary as a receptacle for a poor person infected with a loathsome disease) was set up in 1361 in Harnham – no closer to New Salisbury but now to the south. A feature in the nearby church of St George has long confirmed its presence: a small, concave slit in the western wall of the Trinity Chapel (now Lady Chapel). This is a leper's squint, that allowed sufferers of the disease to observe the priests and the service going on inside whilst remaining safely (at least for those within) outside!

If you lived in Salisbury of old, you stood a good chance of living a shortened life.

AD 1653–1692

TERRIBLE NEWS FROM SALISBURY

Witches Abroad!

SALISBURY'S FIRST-KNOWN CONTRIBUTION to the witchcraft hysteria came centuries before its calamitous low point in the 1600s. In 1159, John of Salisbury (born at Old Sarum, 1115) published his voluminous tome, *Policraticus*, in which he reported on witchcraft in the royal courts and advised royal persons to desist from pagan indulgences. But then he was a bishop!

Perhaps one of the most notorious cases in England occurred in Salisbury 500 years later. Anne Bodenham was servant and mistress to Dr Lamb, astrologer, magician and regarded as something of an expert in the black arts. She soon became known as Dr Lamb's Darling and was eventually tried for witchcraft at Fisherton Anger on 19 March 1653. This is her story.

Anne Bodenham had lived in London for many years when she first met John Lamb. Before long, she was sharing his house as his live-in pupil. His reputation was a constant target for the hysterical minds of the Puritans and on 13 June 1628, he was set upon outside St Paul's Cathedral by an unruly crowd. Lamb had just survived a charge of raping an 11-year-old child, but to the crowd he

was guilty, and Lamb was beaten and stoned to death.

Despite Lamb's grievous reputation, Anne exploited her past connection with the late doctor after moving to Salisbury, claiming her expertise in natural healing and her knowledge of supernatural practices arose from the tutelage of her late companion. One of her most profitable services was to find precious items lost by her many well-to-do clients.

In 1653, Ann Styles, a servant to Richard Goddard of The Close, New Salisbury, became caught up in the theft of a silver spoon from her master and was subsequently accused of attempting to poison two women and planning to break another's neck! In a panic, she

Woodcut of the death of Dr Lamb, 1628. (Author's collection)

confessed, exclaiming all she had done had been on the orders of Bodenham with whom, she claimed, she had studied the arts of the Devil.

It was what many in Salisbury had been waiting for, an opportunity to hang the wild witch whose guilt was 'clear enough' through her past acquaintance with Lamb. Bodenham was arrested and put on trial at the Lent Assizes. During her questioning, she underwent physical interrogation as her tormentors searched for her witch's marks. Two were allegedly found – including one in her 'secret place' – and it should be remembered that by now Anne was an 80-year-old woman. The indignity she felt at such violation can be very easily imagined.

In the end, she confessed to healing the sick through folklore and possessing a deep knowledge of the plants, but denied the many ridiculous accusations against her: such as being able to transform herself into a number of different familiars – cat, dog, lion, bear, wolf, even a bull; that she could launch a person through the air at great speed; and, perhaps most damning for its relevance, that she 'did interfere with Ann Styles by conjuring up the devil who appeared without a head, dressed in black and rented her clothes, tore her skin and tossed her up and down in her chamber'.

Anne was found guilty. She was hanged at Salisbury on 19 March and it is said she went to her death cursing the executioner.

Another who stood trial in Salisbury for witchcraft was Goody Orchard, a woman who moved continuously between Salisbury and the town of Malmesbury. Several claims were made against her, including one that she allegedly caused pain and suffering to a 'young mayde' freshly returned from the fields.

The girl's father had urged her to give food and drink to the wayfaring woman but the belligerent lass refused to do so until she herself had eaten. She had, she said, worked hard whilst this old crone had no doubt been idle these past twelve months!

Goody Orchard thus went into the garden where she supposedly performed a secret ritual using incomprehensible language and returned with a bowl of water, urging the young girl to wash her hands before handling her food. Doing as she was bid, the young girl was instantly struck down with a severe distortion of the hands and fingers and, as soon as Orchard subsequently left, was overcome with a terrible fever. She accused Orchard of being a witch and demanded that she be found and brought back so she could make her well. It took three days to find the older woman, as she begged in the lanes of Edington. She was brought back to the maid's house where she ridiculed the accusation of bewitching the girl. Nevertheless, she took a fresh bowl of water, stirred it three times widdershins (anti-clockwise) and pronounced it clean. The maid sank her aching hands into the cool liquid and found they were instantly cured. Orchard was taken back to Salisbury gaol, tried, convicted and executed as a witch.

Now forgive me for temporarily leaving Wiltshire to cross the Atlantic for Salisbury, Massachusetts, named after our eponymous city. In the days

THE TRYING OF WITCHES

During the monarchy of King James I (James VI of Scotland), trial by water (*indicium aquae*) became prevalent as the king believed it exposed witches: 'the water shall refuse to receive them in her bosom, that have shaken off them the sacred water of baptism and wilfully refused the benefit thereof' (*Barber*, 1988: 151). His Act of 1604 authorised witch hunting and was used to justify the trials at Salem.

Some of the tests for witches included 'swimming' (not to be confused with the ducking stool, which was used with scolds), where the accused woman was bound hand and foot and tossed into the water. The age-old 'if she floats, she's a witch – if she sinks, she was innocent' had found its infamous origins.

One of the more gruesome accounts of 'discovering' witches was written in the fifteenth century by Dominican friars. Much of what appeared in their *Malleus Maleficarum* is too graphic for a book such as this, but some of the 'less offensive' tortures included: forcing boiling water down the throat of the victim, follow by a knotted sheet which, when yanked out, would dislodge the bowels; or binding their thumbs or hands behind their backs and hoisting them up on a pulley to be dropped violently, dislocating the shoulders, elbows and, in some cases, the lower limbs. Other methods included thrawing – tying ropes around the head and jerking it sideways – and burning the groin and armpits with sulphur. All these would take place before the accused had been tried, let alone found guilty!

when North America remained a British colony, the town of Salem lay close to Salisbury and witnessed the most brutal series of witch trials the world has ever known. Susannah Martin, a Salisbury woman, was put on trial in 1692, the year the hysteria reached its bloody peak. She was found 'guilty' of 'seducing' into witchcraft four 'innocent' women and affecting them with magic so that they were 'tortured, afflicted, pined, wasted & tormented'. Her trial, on 29 June, was recorded by Cotton Mather, a Puritan minister at the centre of the persecutions, who accused Martin of being one of the most 'impudent, scurrilous, wicked creatures in the world'.

His testimony included alleged reactions at the beginning of her trial from the four women Martin had allegedly seduced:

As soon as she [Martin] came in, Marcy Lewis and the others had fits.

Magistrate: Do you know this woman?

Abigail Williams: It is goody Martin, she hath hurt me often.

Others by fits were hindered from speaking.

Marcy Lewis pointed at her [Martin] and fell into a little fit.

Ann Putnam threw her glove in a fit at her.

Magistrate (now addressing Martin): What! Do you laugh at it?

Martin: Well I may at such folly.

Magistrate: Is this folly? The hurt of these persons?

Martin: I never hurt man or woman or child.

Marcy: She hath hurt me a great many times and pulls me down.

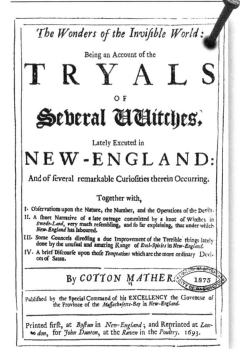

Cotton Mather's account of the Salem trials.
(LC-USZ62-75554)

Mather's record contained other dramatic claims against Susannah. As she stood on trial listening to the fanciful 'evidence', she idly bit her lip. A man in the congregation, seeing the innocent expression, fell down in an uncontrollable fit, crying out: 'That woman – the bites, the bites!'

Others joined in: 'The black man [Satan] is with her!'

Her trial was not only oral. As with most accused witches, she was physically examined in the court room for a 'witch's' tit' – a third nipple from which to feed her familiars. As rough hands removed her shift, she remained stoic and upright until they discovered, as she knew they would, no such aberration. Mather, though, was not to be outdone. He subsequently recorded how her breasts were examined in the morning and found to be full of milk then again in the afternoon when they were seen to sag, as though the milk had been expressed or had been fed to something. GUILTY!

On 19 July, Susannah Martin and four others – Sarah Good, Rebecca Nurse, Elizabeth Howe and Sarah Wilder – were taken to Gallows Hill and strung up by the neck. Their deaths were slow as the long-drop system – whereby the neck broke almost instantly – had not yet been adopted. In total, nineteen men and women were executed in Salem in just fifteen weeks, between June and September. One man, of 81, was 'pressed to death' for refusing to be put on trial, while two dogs were put to death for being witches' familiars!

The final word now must be left to Cotton Mather, who saw a connection between Anne Bodenham of Salisbury, Wiltshire and the women he had put to death in Salem. In his review of the New England trials, he wrote with open hostility of '[t]hat horrid witch of Salisbury who had been servant to the notorious conjurer, Dr Lamb'. Neither Salisbury, Wiltshire nor Salisbury, Massachusetts, would ever know such hysterics again.

AD 1655

A RIGHT ROYAL RUMPUS

A Not-So-Civil War in Salisbury

SALISBURY WAS 'TAKEN' many times during the English Civil War, despite being a relatively unimportant town of no great defensive qualities or political capital. Such were the tentacles of England's last great revolution.

Things at first were tame. In 1642, Prince Maurice marched through Salisbury on his way to join fellow Royalist Commander Hopton, gaining victory in the west. Taking control of the city, he arrested and held the Parliamentarian-supporting mayor for three weeks. Months later, in May 1643, Lord Hertford, another Royalist officer and distant claimant to the throne through his connection to the Seymour family, set up headquarters at Salisbury as he led various successful forays into Somerset and beyond.

But it was in 1644 that Salisbury truly felt the effects of the bloody troubles. In June that year, the Earl of Essex occupied the city as he and his Parliamentary troops made for Lyme Regis; and later Edmund Ludlow, one of the king's fiercest critics and fresh from defeat at Warminster, was pursued through the town by Royalist troops keen on a rout. Rather unwisely, anti-Parliamentarian locals, who were constantly in the minority, hurled abuse and physical brickbats at Ludlow's troop as they attempted to pass. They escaped the rout but Ludlow was so incensed that he returned soon after with a party of horse, extracted a list of those involved and sequestered £200 from the whole damn lot of them!

Later that year the king, celebrating his success in the West Country, established a temporary garrison at

Robert, Earl of Essex. (With kind permission of the Thomas Fisher Rare Book Library, University of Toronto)

THE SALISBURY COMMISSION

The Salisbury Commission that followed Penruddock's Rising included several learned judges, lawyers and magistrates from across the country. In a scene that brings to mind the trial of ex-American Footballer, O.J. Simpson, the selection, deselection and replacement of jurors and even legal counsel was protracted and questionable. At its heart was High Sheriff Dove and the two assizes judges who had suffered personally on the day of the rebellion. Cromwell, though, appears to have recognised the potential for vengeance and insisted on non-local and hopefully less-jaundiced administrators on the board. Nonetheless, the defendants were all found guilty, at least eight lost their lives and many more were forcibly removed from the country they had fought to preserve.

nearby Longford House, with another at Wilton House. As with earlier episodes of the war in Salisbury, it proved short-lived and, in December, the town experienced its fiercest and in truth only serious fighting, lasting until the following January.

Having waited so long for something to happen, and presumably expressing their pent-up frustrations, the people of Salisbury fought bitter hand-to-hand combat. Parliamentarian troops, joined again by the still-irked Ludlow, joined the fray and attacked two regiments of Royalist horse, who quickly barricaded themselves inside the Close. It proved pointless. Ludlow's men burned down the gates and took the officers prisoner, with the others allowed to escape. The victorious Parliamentarians fortified the cathedral belfry and made it their garrison but, that too, proved futile. Not long after being expelled from the city, Royalist troops returned in a surprise attack which led to fierce skirmishes in Market Place, Endless Street and in the Close. They had a score to settle. Attacking the bell tower, they burned down the door and captured those

within. From then, until March 1645, Salisbury had a Royalist hue.

A decade later, in 1655, with Oliver Cromwell now feeling increasingly isolated and Salisbury once again having been left to its Parliamentarian sympathies, the Penruddock Rising was a near farcical attempt at renewing Royalist control. Setting out at dawn on 12 March, Sir John Penruddock, one-time High Sheriff of Wiltshire, led a party of 200 men into Market Place, where they commandeered horses and posted guards in every hostelry. The current high sheriff, Dove, a long-time supporter of Cromwell, was dragged out into the street in just his nightshirt. During unsuccessful attempts to get him to proclaim Charles Stuart as king, the terrified official was pistol-whipped and the blade of a sword used to slice him viciously above the eye. Penruddock's men now wanted to hang the 'rogue' but Sir John himself interceded, seeing more merit in his value as a notable prisoner. It was a decision that would come back to haunt him, as Dove later not only bore witness against him but petitioned the

View of Salisbury, where the armies clashed during the English Civil War. (LC-DIG-ppmsc-08825)

Lord Protector's aides to show no mercy at his future trial.

Salisbury was once again Royalist. The Penruddock Rising, though, failed ever to really win the support of its citizens. Instead, it relied on prisoners freed from Fisherton gaol who (unsurprisingly) pledged their support in exchange for their liberty and the insurrection lasted just two days. Penruddock and 100 men left the city to ride westwards. They were ambushed by Parliamentarian forces in North Devon, interrogated and brought back to Salisbury to be tried for treason.

At the Salisbury Commission, Penruddock confessed to planning the rebellion with likeminded gentlemen of the city and said they had often met in the King's Arms inn to organise the safe return of the exiled Charles II. The date for the rising had been agreed on the suggestion of a mysterious Lady Phillips, recently arrived from London but about whom little else is known. Seven of the rebels were hanged from the city gallows while numerous others were transported for life to the West Indies. Following a protracted and legally doubtful trial, Penruddock was beheaded in Exeter on 16 May, with Cromwell himself signing his death warrant.

However, he would have one last, small victory. Cromwell was now so worried that he appointed major-generals across the country, charged with watching out for future uprisings such as Penruddock had momentarily convened in Salisbury.

AD 1768

THE PEDDLER
AND THE SAILOR

The Cruel Death of Wolf Myers

IN 1768, THE murder of Wolf Myers, a well-known outcast and peddler, touched and shamed every Salisburian who had long held pride in the tolerance and safety of their city.

Monday, 25 January 1768. The snow that had fallen for the past few weeks was hanging around, no doubt portending more to come. The late Christmas-card scene of rolling plains and hidden tracks was, to one unfortunate man, a harbinger of horror. For as he passed the shallow chalk pit by the side of the Coombe road, a small amount of snow had melted in the feeble winter sun to reveal the battered and broken body of one Wolf Myers. Blood was caked hard upon his face, his hands frozen and cracked, while numerous lacerations had rented the skin asunder. Most horrifying of all was that his legs were missing.

The man forced himself to peer closer at the corpse. A halo of stones had been placed around his head, and the low sunlight glinted off something metallic. It was a knife, the blade large and menacing. Was this the weapon that inflicted such awful wounds? He turned and ran, crying out for help.

A few hours later, the dead body was recovered. His legs, in fact, were still attached, but had been buried beneath the obstinate snow. The corpse was carried to a nearby house, where the coroner and his jury soon held their inquest. They confirmed his injuries and crucially the cause of death – struck on the head with a heavy weight, probably a stone. A sharp instrument – the knife – had also lacerated his breast and hands and rented a huge gash that spread upwards from his groin to his belly. There were so many bruises across his body that whoever had killed him had 'done him good'. The coroner's jury reached a decision of wilful murder.

Early inquiries at Salisbury soon identified the victim as a travelling peddler or chapman. He was well known for wandering from town to village with his wooden box upon his back, selling his wares as he went. By some ingenious detection – years before the word was applied to regular police work – his final movements were ascertained. Late on 27 December, a Sunday when trade had been quiet, Wolf made it known he would walk the 2 or so miles to Coombe tomorrow. All he wanted tonight was something to eat and somewhere to lay his head. The Running Horse inn fitted the bill perfectly. The next morning, he

(With kind permission of the Thomas Fisher Rare Book Library, Library of Toronto)

woke early, breakfasted and bid his hosts goodbye. At first he made good progress, passing nobody to slow him down and seeing only the occasional field worker in the distance. Now a quarter-mile from the Coombe turnpike gate, he heard footsteps running behind him.

Before he had a chance to turn around, something solid yet sharp struck the back of his head and his knees buckled.

Falling forward, he hit the chalk path with brutal force. Now in a daze, he felt a knife tear through his coat and penetrate his skin. He attempted to roll over, to fight off the attack, but a second puncture, high above his breast, laid him back, quickly followed by three more, four, five. He flailed at the figure stooping over him, crying out as the blade cut his fingers and punctured his hands. Pinned on his back, his assailant hammered home the advantage, smashing Wolf's pain-wracked body with a huge nodule of flint before plunging the blade deep into his loins and ripping upwards toward his navel. Darkness descended and within seconds, Wolf lay limp. At least the pain had stopped.

On the morning of the coroner's inquest, as many people as possible were questioned, first in Coombe and then in Salisbury. One name was repeatedly offered – John Curtis. The man, it seemed, had appeared late the previous evening covered in blood and bearing atrocious injuries. He claimed to have been robbed on the Blandford road, about 2 miles hence, and horrified locals had taken him

A DYING MAN'S LAST WORDS

John Curtis protested his innocence until the end. As he approached the gallows, he slipped a note to a friend standing beneath the gibbet:

The last dying words of me John Curtis.

I recommend my soul to God, in hopes of pardon and forgiveness for all my sins; as for the crime I am going to die for, I am not guilty, and as I am wronged in this world, I rely upon the mercy of God Almighty to reward me in the next. God Almighty keep everyone from false swearing, and forgive them all as I do, and die in charity with all men.

John Curtis, 27 years of age. March 14th 1768

Hanging in chains was used to humiliate the executed criminal and to serve as a warning to others. John Curtis' body was cut down and hanged again, this time in iron cuffs attached to the gibbet (some towns used an iron cage). Thus he remained *ad infinitum* until the crows had eaten what they wanted and his disarticulated skeleton collapsed in a heap. His bones would then have been buried in unconsecrated ground, usually at a crossroads or, in this case perhaps, near to where he killed his victim.

Occasionally, the criminal was placed in irons and hung whilst alive from a purpose-built frame. Passers-by would often give the unfortunate and starving individual some bread and water, presumably as an act of mercy but, in reality only prolonging an agonising death.

to Salisbury infirmary where he received help with his wounds. It all happened just hours after Wolf Myers' murder and was too much of a coincidence.

Understanding that Curtis was a sailor and had since left for Gosport, the coroner quickly dispatched two people to the Hampshire town where a few enquiries using the man's description soon led them to a 'man-o-war', the *Achilles*. Sure enough, there Curtis was, bearing the wounds he had worn at the infirmary.

The men grabbed him and searched through his possessions where, hidden among the bedding, was a peddlery (a small wooden box carried by men of the road as they touted their wares). Moreover, it contained a little silver, similar if not identical to one or two pieces that the killer had left in Myers' pockets. It was enough. The local magistrate was called for and committed Curtis to the Gosport House of Correction. The following morning, he was taken back to Salisbury and placed in the county gaol. Another search of his belongings discovered some letters in which he complained of being robbed

whilst in Gosport and demanding that the local magistrate, the very same man who had so recently committed him to be detained, should sue the county for his robbery and loss.

Instead, John Curtis, actually a Portuguese man called Courtine, stood trial at the Assizes on 5 March, where he was found guilty of the brutal murder. Two weeks later, ahead of his execution, he was taken back to the chalk pit and asked if he recalled what had happened there. He replied in the negative. A little later, as he climbed the gallows, he slipped a note to a friend in the crowd. It vehemently maintained his innocence to the end (*see* text box). Curtis was hanged as sentenced and soon after, his body was hung in chains (*see* text box) near the spot where the murder occurred.

Meanwhile, the body of Wolf Myers was recovered by friends and family from London and taken back for burial. As was the custom, a copper medallion was struck to mark his cruel death and placed near the spot where he was so brutally killed. A second disc recorded the family's satisfaction that John Curtis, cowardly killer, had been executed.

AD 1810–1865
IN GOD WE TRUST!

Gaols and Gallows

UNFORTUNATE FISHERTON, AS well as having a lunatic asylum (*see* next chapter), also housed the county gaol and, from no later than 1611, hosted public executions at a spot known as Gallows Gate, shown on Speed's map of that date. The crimes and executions were so numerous and varied that only a meagre few can be featured here ...

Dumb and dumber

In the summer of 1810, two young men – Thomas Jones (alias Hughes) and Richard Francis – robbed a Salisbury jeweller, making off with a large swag of watches, chains, seals and items of gold and silver. Days later, they committed a further act so incredibly stupid it could only ever have one outcome.

The Taunton–London coach had reached Sutton Scotney, about 25 miles from Fisherton, when two men carrying a large bundle emerged from behind a hedge. The coachman recognised them immediately, for as the vehicle had travelled through Salisbury that morning, gossip about the crime and descriptions of the two men had reached his ears. Confiding in one of his other passengers, the pair discreetly alerted

the police during their next scheduled stop, at Egham in Surrey, The two felons were arrested on the spot and taken on to London, to the home of the Bow Street Runners. In time, the jeweller was able to confirm the items inside the bundle were indeed those that had been stolen some days before and the men were brought back to Salisbury. At the ensuing Assizes, the court heard how Jones was in fact an escaped convict and decided the pair were guilty as charged. Both were sentenced to hang.

Francis approached his fate with religious fervour and died stoically as a penitent. Jones, though, remained belligerent. As he took to the scaffold, the rope already around his neck, he tossed his hat into the crowd and facetiously thanked them for turning up!

Plaque marking the spot of the old Fisherton gaol. (David J. Vaughan)

Owing to some complication with the rope, coupled with the man's light frame, he took many long, painful minutes to die. His arrogance – and stupidity – lost finally as he struggled to take his last breath.

It was the drink that did it!

In 1834, the demon drink led a man to his execution. Charles Kimmer, 28, had set fire to some hay ricks in nearby Oare, a crime for which he swung on the gallows. A habitual drinker, Kimmer had spent his considerable wages as a regular in the public houses and beer shops lying between Salisbury and the scene of his impromptu conflagration. When arrested, he at last confessed his crime to the local church minister, during which he reportedly turned very pale and suffered the cold sweats, tearing at both his clothes and flesh. Bloodied and bowed, he was taken before the magistrate and thence to the Assizes where he was duly sentenced to hang, and returned to Fisherton gaol.

On the eve of his execution, he turned his hope again to God. The prison chaplain, somewhat unhelpfully, preached from the Book of Timothy: 'The time of thy departure is at hand'!

Kimmer was then asked if he would die with his irons on, to which he answered simply: 'Yes.' As he was brought forward for the drop, he spoke to a crowd numbering many hundreds. He implored them to turn from the evils of drink, and the breaking of the Sabbath, for it had brought him here. With his words fresh on his lips, the rope snapped tight and Charles Kimmer was plunged below and into eternity. The local brew houses too mourned a drop – in their profits.

The Salisbury poisoning case

Not all inmates of the gaol hung around for the hangman's noose. In 1865, William Storer, a surgeon's assistant, had been committed to stand trial for poisoning his sweetheart, Emily Blake, daughter of a Salisbury surgeon and Storer's employer. He denied the crime violently, claiming that Emily had taken more strychnine than he had prescribed for her chronic menstruation pains. Nevertheless, his case began and by the time matters came to a head, he had spent three long months in Fisherton gaol, with a further three to endure before his trial at the Lent Assizes. It was more than he could bear.

The dreadful state of the poor man's mind is evident in the three suicide notes that were found in his cell ... the first was his account of the death of dearest Emily, in which he again asserted his innocence. He also made claims of cruelty by the gaol governor, including the overzealous use of the refractory cells and the punishment diet of bread and water. His second letter, addressed to his aunts, displayed the warning signs of a weakening mind: 'This is a dreadful life to lead that one gets here.' This note ended abruptly, mid-sentence. The final letter was addressed to nobody in particular, but announced his intention to escape this harsh life, using the only means open to him. It began almost as a rant:

> No! Little did I think that Emily Sophia Blake would have taken four of the pills I gave her, or she would not have had them. I loved her ... and knowing as I do that I should get an acquittal if I stood the test of an earthly trial, yet I cannot live with a broken heart another three months

BOUND TO SUFFER

Perhaps no punishment bestowed on criminals was more abhorrent than the giving of permission to carry out anatomical dissection. Often the medical officer entrusted to perform the operation separately arranged for the victim's skin to be stripped off and used as the binding for a fitting book – the account of the crime itself. This grisly practice, formally called anthropodermic bibliopegy, was especially popular in the seventeenth to nineteenth centuries and, from the recorded cases of that period, John Horwood's in 1821 was one of the better known.

Horwood was unlucky. He was executed for murdering his one-time sweetheart after throwing a stone in a fit of jealousy and catching her on the temple. At first she was only injured but then a doctor at the Bristol Royal Infirmary operated on a

Dissection class in the sixteenth century, showing the type of dissecting room common up until the practice died out three centuries later. (LC-USZ62-95233)

depressed fracture of the skull. As he did, an abscess formed and the girl was dead in less than a week. Horwood was charged and at his trial, the same doctor testified against him! Inevitably perhaps, he was sentenced to death. The judge ordered that his body be returned to the (same) doctor for dissection, the medic taking it upon himself to remove Horwood's skin, tan it and use it to bind the papers from the trial. Cruelly, these included letters from John's parents pleading with the doctor to return their son's body for a decent burial. In a final macabre twist, he instead kept the skeleton at home!

Early in 2011, John Horwood's mortal remains were rediscovered hanging pitifully in a cupboard at Bristol University, where the noose remained wrapped around his neck! In April that year, he was at last given the decent burial the culpable doctor had denied him. He was interred alongside his father exactly 190 years to the hour since he had died on the gallows.

---

in this gaol. I feel that my Saviour will forgive me my past sins, and now I go to Him. Rest! Rest! W.J.S December 12

William Storer's body was discovered face down in the prison bath. His hands were behind his back, tied with a torn piece of cloth. It transpired later that he had previously tried to persuade a warder to bring him poison for his own use. He was the first inmate to allegedly commit suicide in the new Fisherton gaol.

William's body was interred at midnight without religious service – typical 'punishment' for suicide victims. Unfortunately, the trust in God he pronounced in his final letter did not attract any compassion from the earthbound authorities at Fisherton gaol.

AD 1813–1954

THE DEAD AND THE MAD

Fisherton House Lunatic Asylum

VICTORIAN ASYLUMS ARE now seen as either a hidden piece of a city's dark history or as an optimistic move by far-sighted philanthropists. Fisherton House in Salisbury fitted the bill in both cases.

Background

Fisherton had originally been the brainchild of Charles Finch, doctor and local worthy, who conceived the idea of a private institution for fee-paying patients. It opened in 1813 and by 1850 began receiving criminal lunatics, largely to alleviate chronic overcrowding in the notorious Bethlem hospital.

The house, in fact a sizeable range of buildings, was located on the secluded site of what had probably once been the original manor house. Society still preferred to keep its less controllable members away from the denser populations of busy towns, while the surrounding area, gentrified since the turn of the century, reflected the latest preference for a quieter location and gentler design.

By 1856, Fisherton had become the largest privately run mental hospital in England, with some 700 beds and well in excess of 100 criminal inmates, transferred from prisons across the country. Inevitably, it brought some interesting people and numerous undesirable events ...

The hunting of the snark

With such a collection of troubled minds and violent souls, it was unsurprising that many were associated with murder, attempted murder or intemperance; which didn't stop once they reached Fisherton House! In 1873, Robert Skeffington Lutwidge (favoured Uncle Skeffington of author Lewis Carroll) stepped into his own wonderland when he visited the asylum as esteemed secretary of the new Lunacy Commission.

William McKave had been a patient for more than twenty years, having lost repeated appeals to be removed to another asylum. When Skeffington and his fellow commissioner arrived on 21 May, McKave saw an opportunity to make his point. Having feigned sleep as the men passed by, he leapt suddenly to his feet and launched himself at Skeffington. An iron nail secreted in his hand entered the poor man's temple as he drove home the makeshift weapon.

Lewis Carroll. (Library of Congress LC-USZ62-70064)

Skeffington, who had fallen to the floor, was raced to the director's quarters and from there to the White Hart hotel, where emergency treatment was sought. Lewis Carroll received word of the attack and rushed to his uncle's bedside. No sooner had he arrived than the injured man appeared to rally and Lewis returned to London much relieved. A few hours later, however, his uncle weakened again and soon after slipped away. The nail, it seemed, had penetrated his brain.

Long after this tragic event, there have been disputed claims that it became the inspiration behind Carroll's nonsense poem, 'The Hunting of the Snark'. Carroll himself always rejected the idea.

Almost Sullivan but no Gilbert

One anonymous male inmate, a one-time successful businessman, almost denied Britain the operatic genius of Gilbert and Sullivan. William Gilbert was also a barrister, having a special interest in the debates on insanity and crime. Having visited Fisherton House in 1863, he wrote about his experience some time later. An unnamed gentleman had been a criminal patient, incarcerated after he murdered a tax collector who had attempted to serve him with a summons for failing to have a dog license. The man approached Gilbert, wishing to present his case for being set free. In short, he argued, he should be released, as the killing of any man who insisted that keeping a dog should mean paying a tax had been totally justified!

Rather foolishly, Gilbert rebuffed the claim, asserting that his crime was made no less wicked than if the tax collector had been chasing him for a rent on his home. 'No matter' said Gilbert, 'you are bound to pay the tax for a dog as well as a house.'

'Is that really your opinion?' the man replied, becoming agitated.

'Certainly.'

'Very well, I shall know you whenever I see you again and if ever I get from here, I will rip you up as I did the tax-gatherer!'

Gilbert was led quickly to another room in the asylum.

Hell hath no fury

It was not only men who threatened violence at the slightest provocation. Indeed, violence and women went hand in hand at Fisherton in many of the cases.

Mary Ann Ball was a specialist. In her twenties and regarded as attractive, she was inordinately vain and preserved her appearance with obvious relish. She would fight anyone who forced her to conform to mundane uniformity, and she had the strength and bite of a tigress. While in prison, she was wont to be incarcerated in the punishment cell whenever she felt an insane

A derelict Fisherton House Lunatic Asylum.
(David J. Vaughan)

episode coming upon her and every incarceration was accompanied with a temper so violent she ripped up the gratings and stone floor. Even handcuffs and the straitjacket were ineffective as she tore them off!

Here at Fisherton, she was controlled not with savage strength but by responding to the two or three hour period of sullenness which always preceded her violent outbursts. At such times, the staff administered a drug to create nausea just sufficient to keep her 'tame' until the episode had passed.

One of the most infamous female criminal lunatics under Fisherton's roof was Celestina Sommer who, in 1856, took her only daughter into the cellar of her London home and slit her throat. At first sentenced to hang, she later received a commutation to penal servitude for life, during which her obvious insanity came to light and she was duly transferred in 1858 to Fisherton House. Such was her international notoriety, the subject of parliamentary and media interest, that by the time she came to Salisbury she was one of the most hated women in Victorian Britain. Surprising, then, that by the staff and patients alike she was considered one of the most gentle,

obedient inmates the asylum had ever treated. She died in 1859, taking the truth behind her insanity with her.

Along with so many others, she was one of a who's who of celebrity killers who spent their last days on earth in the warm embrace of Fisherton House.

Tools of the trade

In the centre of the male criminal ward, amidst some of the most violent and troubled inmates in the entire asylum, sat a cruel-looking cage complete with small camp bed and lockable door. But this was no primitive form of restraint: it was the night warder's bed. When the time came for him to take some rest, the officer clambered in, locked himself inside and rested safe in the knowledge that he would reach daylight without his throat being cut.

And talking of cutting throats ... one particular patient in the asylum took great affront at something innocuous uttered by one of the warders. In a clear demonstration of the dangers of working in a nineteenth-century asylum, the man exacted revenge by sharpening an iron hoop and, fixing it to a wooden handle, ripped the neck of the said warder, narrowly missing his carotid artery – the one which supplies blood to the brain. To have severed it would have meant certain death.

Macabre spectacles

One of the most popular events for the inmates of Fisherton was the regular 'Lunatics' Ball'. Considered a 'freak show' by many, it took place in the single-storey building that once lay opposite the main entrance. Extending to some 60 or 70ft, the building contained an orchestra 'pit'

THE LADY BURNS

—⊶⊷—

A tragedy befell Fisherton House on 4 March 1907, when 71-year-old Jane Hobbs wandered into the kitchen of Ward 19 and somehow set herself on fire. On seeing smoke pouring from a window, two nurses ran to the room to find the elderly patient sat quite still at the table, her clothes alight and her face obscured by the fierce flames. Her shawl, it seemed, had caught the small fire in the nearby grate.

Acting quickly, the two women quelled the flames with blankets and called for the medical superintendent; who attended to the poor woman's extensive injuries where she sat. She was severely burned, particularly about the neck, arms and hands, and unsurprisingly passed away a few hours later. The coroner's inquest returned a verdict of 'Accidental Death', though the coroner questioned whether the door to the kitchen should be locked, and the foreman enquired whether a larger fireguard would have prevented the tragedy.

—⊶⊷—

– actually situated 10ft from the ground – a piano, and had lighting provided by the recently installed gas-lamps.

Singing and dancing was held every week and, on special occasions, magicians and storytellers performed star turns. But it was the ballroom which made for the most unusual display. Men and women – murderers, burglars, private fee-paying clients, poisoners, drunkards – all sat in rigid lines, facing one another from opposite walls, until the band (all warders) struck up a tune and excited a response.

The 'gallant' males courteously approached the 'flattered' women and asked them to dance the quadrille or the mazurka. Their rigid, awkward movements presented a pitiable parody and, once the music had stopped, everyone returned to their seats and waited for the next tune. It all resembled a clockwork toy, constantly in need of the key.

Yet not all of the shows were quite so orderly. The performance of *Hamlet*, including the pivotal moment when a murder is committed, drove the audience into uproar and threatened to erupt into riot; even though many of them had been committed for exactly that crime! Indeed, the one who showed the strongest objection had been incarcerated at Fisherton after cutting off his doctor's head and kicking it about the garden!

Closed doors

Fisherton House was hailed by many to be the 'model' asylum, far removed both physically and aesthetically from the previously feared institutions. It remained a privately run home until 1954, when it continued as a mental hospital under the local National Health Service. It closed again in the 1990s, when the building was finally abandoned. It has since sat in a neglected corner of a modern development, as isolated and lost as the hundreds of patients it once housed.

AD 1830

IF ONLY THERE WAS CAKE TO EAT!

The Salisbury Swing Riots

IN RECALLING THE phrase often attributed to Marie Antoinette's dismissive response to the plight of the starving French peasants, the Swing Riots of the early nineteenth century were a violent part of rural uprisings by the equally desperate British farm workers. Salisbury was caught up in the troubles and, in particular, the unjust trials that followed in its Guildhall, newly extended and thus able to accommodate the large number of defendants.

The rural rebellion, which had begun in Kent, spread south and west as quickly as the fires lit by the protestors. They reached Wiltshire within days. Soon, it had become one of the most vociferous of the counties involved, unsurprising given its reliance on an agricultural economy. The political commentator, William Cobbett, during his visitation to the region, described the workers' conditions here as the worst he had ever known. It was shameful, he exclaimed, for an Englishmen to see the poverty and ruthless conditions under which these people strived and failed to make a living. He concluded that the predictable end 'will be dreadful'. And he was soon proved right. After two failed harvests, rampant

The hated horse-powered threshing machine. (THP)

starvation and continued oppression, the final straw came with the introduction of the newfangled threshing machine which put desperate people out of work. The rural population were soon in revolt and fighting quickly spread along the Wylye Valley.

On 25 November, in Tisbury, hundreds of agricultural labourers gathered in the village carrying various weapons – sticks, stones, even iron bars. Despite the pleadings of the largest landowner, the crowd splintered into three groups and, between them, tore down a barn, wrecked the hated machines which so threatened their livelihood and attacked the man. A heavy stone thrown from the rabble caught him between the eyes, drawing a great deal of blood.

The militia were summoned to restore order yet, despite arriving with their sabres drawn and held aloft, the rioters stood their ground. Mass brawls broke out and many men suffered atrocious injuries – one lost three fingers from his left hand and a further two from his

A potential rioter being tempted into burning. (Author's collection)

right; another suffered a slash so deep it cut through his muscle; and yet one more lost a piece of his skull, sliced clean off. One of the yeomanry suddenly drew his revolver and fired. The bullet passed straight through John Harding's brain, the poor man collapsing to the floor. He was the first fatality of the Swing Riots in England.

Soon after, the militia brought the crowd under control and many were arrested and carted off to Salisbury. A further nineteen were picked up in Wilton where they had simultaneously rioted. A wagon load of injured and broken men were taken either to the infirmary or to Fisherton gaol, where a party of Lancers was situated to prevent further trouble.

Even before the tragic events that night, more riots had occurred in and around Salisbury, such as at Bishop's Down Farm, just two days before, and at nearby Hindon. They also targeted a local farmer who possessed a mechanical thresher. During the mêlée he was struck on the head by a hammer thrown from the crowd and the tool-turned-weapon was identified as belonging to a shoemaker. He was arrested on this weakest of circumstantial evidence and transported for life.

After the tribulations, the trial

The trials of the Tisbury Swing Rioters took place at the Guildhall on New Year's Day, 1831. Tensions ran high, and worsened when the foreman of the jury turned out to be the very landowner they had attacked, and two of the jurors were members of the militia who had arrested those brought before the court! The defendants' fears of injustice

REASONS TO SWING

⁓

The Swing Riots were centred on workers' pay decreasing and conditions worsening at exactly the same time that saw landowner profits increase. Many workers lived below the breadline and saw their already meagre income further eroded by the introduction of the mechanised threshing machine. Since fields had been enclosed toward the end of the previous century, workers had lost regular employment to seasonal work and even the tied cottages they once lived in were taken from them, as the local landlord no longer needing to house his staff all year round. Workhouses and poor houses filled up at an alarming rate.

⁓

were well founded: twenty-three were transported, fourteen of them for life. At the same time, the killing of John Harding was dismissed as lawful homicide, on the grounds that he had in effect committed *felo de se* (suicide) by putting himself in such a position as would lead to his death! In recognition of the rioters' plight, a plaque was unveiled inside the Guildhall in 2011, on the site of their worst suffering.

A contemporary engraving. (Author's collection)

Things were worse around the county. One hundred and fifty-two prisoners were transported, fifty-seven were gaoled and one unfortunate was hanged. Nationally, some 252 were originally sentenced to death, with 232 were subsequently commuted to transportation for life. No less than nineteen people were executed – including a 12-year-old boy – some 500 were transported overseas (again, many of them for life) and even more were imprisoned.

The Swing Riots in Salisbury had been put down with a ferocity only matched in the cruel circumstances leading up to the troubles. Just four years later, they erupted again, this time in Tolpuddle, Dorset.

Which only leaves an explanation for the term 'Swing Riots'. The name came from a series of threatening letters sent to landowners and institutions, demanding improved pay and conditions. It claimed that, if these were not forthcoming, the recipients would see their properties burned, the much-hated threshing machines destroyed and have to endure great personal suffering. Each letter, regardless of its geographical origin, was signed by Captain Swing – a fictitious name – since interpreted as not just an attempt at anonymity, but a veiled threat to a more sickening punishment if the originators of the letters were not taken seriously.

AD 1849
FILTH AND FILTHABILITY

Open Sewers and
the Great Cholera Outbreak

OUTSIDE THE NEW cathedral and Close, Salisbury laid out its commercial and residential centre in a grid pattern, known locally as the Chequers. Similar to a chess board, its twenty regular(ish) squares were each given a different name and water courses were built to demarcate each plot. These open channels provided drinking water for the town's earliest inhabitants but, with a high water table just below the surface, they soon brought death and suffering to the people of this once-called 'promised land'.

New Salisbury had in fact been built on extensive floodplains and the damp conditions, together with early trades and lifestyles, quickly produced a cesspool of rank detritus. Today's St Ann Street was once known as Tanner Row (Author: having once worked opposite a tannery, I can imagine the smell!); New Street Chequer included wells, drains and yard surfaces; Brown Street has produced evidence of filleting and the smoking of fish and butchery, as well as discarded horn cores; and, more recently, Culver Street has produced two thirteenth-century cesspits. Other road names include: Fish Row, Salt Lane, Butcher

Speed's map, 1611. (Author's collection)

Row; and Poultry, Cheese and Milk Crosses complete the picture.

The Chequers were enclosed by three main ditches, Town, Close and Hussey, which were left open as late as the nineteenth century, producing a cocktail of disease and ill health. In 1870, Town Ditch contained human and animal waste from the Middle Ages, and Hussey's Ditch was found to have been situated near to a butcher's and a carcass-processing site, the effluent discharged into the Chequers' streams. Finally, human burials from the post-Medieval period were interred in the middle of this filth in poisonous lead coffins, creating an unhealthy stew that oozed underfoot. If the stench didn't kill you ... The main problem of course was that all this effluent had only one place to go – straight into the watercourses.

Whilst the date of the Chequers' construction remains uncertain, their antiquity and function as Salisbury's sewers is beyond doubt and the cholera outbreak of 1849 was a disaster waiting to happen. Almost 200 people died and more than 1,300 cases were reported to the infirmary on Fisherton Street. The source of the mortal disease was not hard to find: cesspits and putrid wells stagnated next to each other, clogged with the outpourings of Salisbury's bowels, and turgid sludge choked by decaying animal matter seeped along the open watercourses, with the air rank and fetid water backing up in the narrow channels, spilling out onto the streets. Unbelievably, though, there was great resistance to putting things right from the town administrators.

An early 'solution' saw hatches placed in an effort to dam this scummy tide, but they only created piles of solid matter which had to be heaved onto the pavements and allowed to dry before being collected! The first warning of an impending cholera outbreak came in 1847, when the pupils and teachers at Godolphin School for orphaned Christian girls had to relocate from the Close to Milford Hill.

By now, the water table had risen still higher as the subsoil, acting like a giant sponge, soaked up the foul matter and turned the surface into a mat, preventing new emissions from soaking away. The diseased waters, as thick as soup, were now so deep that new graves being dug in St Mark's cemetery were instantly filled up with this fluid filth.

By 1849, scores of people now suffering from cholera were transferred to the isolation hospital at Bugmore. It was not the brightest move, as a place less suited to recovery is hard to imagine. 'Boggy-moor' was a wet area, continuously used for draining the water courses and both the Town and Close ditches. It was forever flooded and yet here successively stood a workhouse, a pest-house and the smallpox hospital, which later became the isolation hospital. Two years after the cholera outbreak, it was described as 'a small, ill-built and dilapidated house with a gable roof overhanging the open sewer'.

Meanwhile, the sewage-filled channels continued to serve as Salisbury's drinking water and the fine citizens were now so used to its taste and 'quality' that they publicly lauded it as sweet tasting! At least, that is, until someone pointed out that this was due to the inherent human excrement. No wonder, 130 years later, John Chandler, whose seminal work on the subject provided much of the information for this chapter, proclaimed: 'The proud and prosperous city of 1420 had become by 1620 [and evidently still was by 1849] a place of squalour, poverty and plague.'

Salisbury's saviour was Andrew B. Middleton, a local doctor whose efforts to improve the townsfolks' health were initially met with derision. He found Bugmore particularly objectionable, citing eight cottages whose inhabitants washed themselves and their clothes in sewage-filled water spewing from the drain outside. They had erected a communal privy from old bits of matting

CHOLERA IN BRITAIN

The Salisbury outbreak was just a small part of the epidemic sweeping Britain in 1849. One of the first people to die included the aptly named Isabella Hazard, a 12-year-old girl from Sunderland (*see* illustration). Her death, like all sufferers, came quickly. The signs included the so-called 'blue stage', by which time death was imminent, and symptoms included watery diarrhoea (leading to acute dehydration, one of the main causes of death); aching muscles; vomiting; and liquid stools that contained tiny whitish flakes from the intestine wall and gave it the appearance of rice water. By then, there was no hope of recovery.

No one knew what caused the illness, and early treatments included brandy and a tobacco enema! Ignorant and afraid, entire towns and cities went into lockdown to try and curb the disease's spread. In Liverpool, panic over grave robbers moving infected corpses led to the so-called Cholera Riots of 1832, in which individuals suspected of either carrying the disease or of stealing infected bodies were attacked in the street.

Progress was eventually made when scientists linked the affliction with over-crowding and poor sanitation. Though it was not until Louis Pasteur in 1864 and Robert Koch in 1883 that the disease was finally understood. By then, it had claimed the lives of over half of those infected and 33,000 lives in Britain during one three-month period alone.

Isabella Hazard. (Author's collection)

---

and leather, and placed it against a wall on the public thoroughfare where it could overhang the open sewer!

Middleton's efforts were strenuously resisted by the city aldermen who, owning most of the land, saw unnecessary expense in curing the problem. At last though, in 1852, his recommended improvements were finally enacted. It was four years after the country's new Public Health Act allowed ratepayers' money to be used to fund improvements in sanitation and two years before John Snow proved the link between cholera and dirty water. The public waterworks opened in 1854 and the notorious watercourses were filled in. The townsfolk were so grateful towards Middleton that a stained-glass window was installed in the cathedral, largely in recognition of his pioneering work.

The city had never had it so good. Salisbury no longer needed to drink its own filth!

AD 1879

THE CURSE OF THE ELEPHANT AND CASTLE

Suicides in Salisbury

EVERYBODY KNOWS THE dangers of drink, but for some people an association with the former Elephant and Castle inn at Ox-Row was decidedly fatal. In just eighteen years, there were no less than five suicides, all but one committed on the premises, the other acted out nearby in carbon copy style.

The earliest known tragedy happened around 1862, though the circumstances remain unknown. A second, by a man called Croom, occurred soon after, but records have never been found. The third – and first to be clearly recorded – involved 32-year-old Mary Batten, wife of the landlord, Alfred.

'When you want me, call'

On the morning of 11 August 1877, Mary Batten, mother of five of whom the youngest was barely 1, went downstairs to the kitchen at the back of the public house and engaged there with the servant, Matilda Ewence. Carrying a child on each hip, she still managed to draw a shaking hand across her damp forehead. 'Oh Jane [*sic*], how queer I feel in my head.'

She had complained for many weeks of bad headaches, seemingly without any obvious cause, and Matilda had grown increasingly worried. She suggested that she take the younger child and put him down to sleep, leaving Mary grateful to be carrying just the older infant. She went through to the bar where her husband was preparing for the day's business.

'When you want me,' she said, 'call me,' and returned upstairs to lie down.

Matilda put the youngster in his cot and then went to Mary's room to check on her mistress. She could get no answer. Tentatively opening the door, she saw the older child laid out on the bed, his mother beside him. Then she saw a large pool of blood and a scarlet-stained razor neatly placed on the hearth, some 18in away. She turned and fled, screaming out for Mr Batten to come at once. As soon as Alfred saw his dear wife, he yelled at the girl to fetch a surgeon.

Dr Gordon arrived within minutes. Try as he might, he could find no pulse. But then Mary's eyes moved and looked at him, full of pity. Instinctively, he held her in his arms, her head turning so that he saw how the throat had been cut from ear to ear, clearly by her own hand. She had severed the carotid artery and even sliced through her larynx. Moments later, Mary's body went limp.

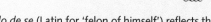

FELO DE SE

Felo de se (Latin for 'felon of himself') reflects the unsympathetic attitudes to suicide that existed in Victorian and earlier England. This somewhat judgmental term was used to explain the temporary insanity which the unfortunate victim suffered as he or she carried out the dreadful deed. Such assumptions subsequently had an effect on the practicalities of life after death, and even today suicide negates the payment of life insurance as self-induced harm.

Perhaps worse still was how society responded to suicide when burying the corpse. Death by one's own hand was seen not just as a criminal deed (against oneself) but an act of sin in the eyes of God: no one but He could take away life. Consequently, suicide victims could not be buried in God's consecrated ground and were often interred at points of uncertain direction – at crossroads or near the village boundary: betwixt and between.

Suffer little children

Before the second anniversary of Mary Batten's awful death, Alfred, who had remained landlord and had now remarried, went into the cellar one morning to change the barrels. After failing to return, a servant went down to check on his employer and found him hanging from an overhead beam. The 'rope', actually a piece of hemp retrieved from his bed, had been knotted through the staple driven into the archaic timber. So low was the ceiling that his feet touched the floor, his corpse hanging in a contorted, semi-crouched position. Alfred had evidently held himself raised at the knees, until the pressure on his throat carried him into eternal darkness.

At the inquest, it transpired that Alfred had behaved strangely in recent weeks. He had been unusually violent towards his second wife and had been seen dancing manically up and down the street outside the pub. On another occasion, he had gone out in the evening not to return until 6 a.m.

with no account of where he had been or what he had done. During one particularly odd episode, he had been missing for a few days when a telegram arrived at the pub from Aldershot with instructions on ordering beer from the brewer. Alfred was recorded as the sender.

Sometime later, he sent a £5 postal order to his mother with orders to use it to look after his children. On 11 July 1879, Alfred Batten had killed himself on the same premises as his wife two years before, almost to the day.

Copycat death

Tragically this was by no means the end of the pub's curse. The next recorded tragedy occurred just two weeks later, on 25 July 1879, in near-identical circumstances. Thomas Coleman, 27, a local florist, had been complaining for a number of weeks of severe pains in his head. During the past fortnight, he had become unhealthily fascinated with Alfred Batten's death, in particular the method of his suicide.

His grisly obsession showed itself in both the time and means of his own self-murder.

To the exact hour of the day as Alfred, he drove a staple into a piece of timber, threaded through a piece of rope and hanged himself, his legs drawn up so that his weight was taken by the neck. The only difference was that he had committed the act not on the pub premises but outside, in the full glare of probable discovery. A small box on which he had stood lay kicked away beside his body.

Even more mysterious was that it seemed to be an impromptu act. He still wore his hat and his shirt sleeves were rolled up, as though, the doctor said at the time, he was in the middle of his work when the urge took him.

Five suicides then were known to have occurred in direct connection with the Elephant and Castle. Yet even now, there are rumours of a sixth, thought to have happened twenty years before the first. If true, it would make the awful history of the inn even more miserable.

AD 1880–1906

'FOR GOD'S SAKE, COME AND HELP US!'

Death and Destruction in Salisbury

TRAIN TRAVEL WAS intended to bring freedom and efficiency to Salisbury. Great Western Railway (GWR) in 1856 and London & South West Railway (L&SWR) in 1859 both opened lines and stations on routes between London and the south coast. Within months, however, there were fatalities, as men, women and children were killed by unseen trains, industrial negligence or, in two horrific crashes, from travelling at great speed.

1884: Breamore disaster

In the sunlight of a June evening, the train on the Salisbury–Dorset line approached an infamous 'S' bend about 200 yards beyond the river when it began to rattle and shake violently. Panic spread through the seven carriages and a sense of doom descended over the passengers. Being market day in Salisbury, the number of people crowding the train for home was unusually excessive.

Suddenly, the middle car jumped the rails and flew down the embankment, crashing into the water-filled ditch below, and other cars decoupled from the engine. Timber from the walls and roofs splintered like firewood and the sides opened up like cheap tin cans

as carriages toppled left and right. The noise of the injured and dying was woeful. Sobs were heard from somewhere deep within the carnage, while morbid, wailing groans vacillated with fierce cries for help. Then, eerily, for a moment all fell silent. Seconds later, screams again filled the air, now heavy with steam, smoke and the crackling of burning timbers.

The first lucky survivors climbed through the broken windows, some even through the gaping holes in the carriage walls. Help began to arrive from other stations but, in particular, from the nearby Agricultural College at Downton, where permission was given to take the dead, the lecture hall being used as a temporary morgue. A telegram was dispatched to the Salisbury infirmary to prepare for the injured. In one awful case, the stationmaster from an adjacent halt arrived to see a dead body trapped in the water beneath a broken carriage. He pulled it free but on turning it over looked straight into the eyes of his 14-year-old daughter. Her lifeless body bore no injuries and it was apparent that she, like others, had died from drowning.

Salisbury was in terrible mourning. Yet it knew the death toll of five could

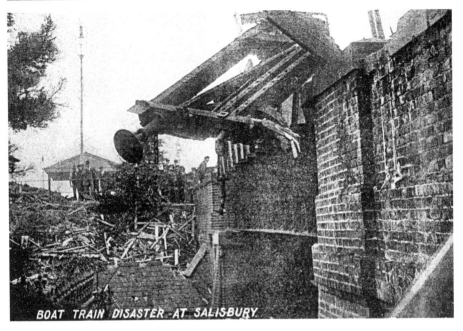

BOAT TRAIN DISASTER AT SALISBURY.

(Courtesy of the Wiltshire and Swindon History Centre)

have been much greater, and in 1906, it was ...

1906: Salisbury Station

Just after 2 a.m. on 1 July, Salisbury's worst rail accident in history occurred on the line as it left the city station and headed north-east for London. The boat train brought American passengers from their liner, SS *New York*, moored at Plymouth. Though smaller than its 1884 predecessor, in both length and number of carriages, the death toll was enormous – twenty-eight killed and scores more injured.

In the dark and deserted station, the boat train to London rushed past the platform at twice the speed it should have – a phenomenal 70mph, the inquest later calculated. Crossing the bridge over Fisherton Street, the train tried to negotiate the sharp left-hand curve in the track, only it would never make it.

As it hit the bend, the leading engine left the tracks and jackknifed, careering along the track at right angles. Carriages behind it flew past, lifting above the rails.

A milk train, which had trundled into the station in the opposite direction, bore the full force. Wood smashed and disintegrated, its wagons scattering like nine-pins. In the last wagon of the eight, the guards van, the occupant died instantly as, at the other end, its engine erupted in a pall of steam and metal. The boat train's engine, meanwhile, raced on, hitting the lattice ironwork of the bridge with hideous force and ricocheted back through the debris, striking the stationary engine of a goods train. The fireman and driver of the latter suffered horrific burns from the escaping steam, but their colleagues on the express fared worse – killed outright. Behind them, one of the wrecked carriages flew straight into Fisherton Street bridge.

It rose up above the parapet and hung there, beyond the railings, threatening to fall at any moment and the bridge with it. One unfortunate passenger was thrown through a hole in the carriage wall and fell 40ft to the roadside below. He was dead on impact.

Another carriage passed its now dislocated engine, and leapt up onto the roof of what had once been the lead car, crushing its passengers beneath. For a long time thus, 'the living were imprisoned with the dead'. This was truly Hell on Earth.

The fireman of the stationary goods train, Chick, showed immense courage when he refused a stretcher and walked, or crawled, all the way to the infirmary, insisting others were in greater need of assistance than he. Arriving at the hospital, his skin reportedly fell off, so bad were his scalds, and within two hours the selfless fireman had died.

Once again, Salisbury responded with remarkable spirit. The impact in the early hours of the quiet Sunday morning had resounded like an earthquake, many fearing exactly that until they heard the whoosh of escaping steam. Those first to arrive on the scene saw a passenger, his head craned through the shattered window, call with a voice full of pain and terror: 'For God's sake, come and help us!'

The injured were soon being led or carried from the wreckage, while platforms were piled high with pathetic refuse – cutlery, upholstery, seats, shattered timbers, doors, windows, glass, twisted iron. The waiting rooms in the station were laid out with dead bodies.

The gloom of the early hour made rescue efforts difficult, as torches and lamps were used to cast insufficient light on the awful scene. It was well into the afternoon when nine more bodies were

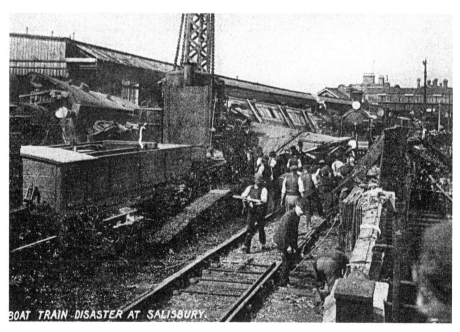

BOAT TRAIN DISASTER AT SALISBURY.

(Courtesy of the Wiltshire and Swindon History Centre)

PERSONAL TRAGEDY

―∞∞―

As well as the awful crashes, the arrival of the railway brought individual tragedy. In 1880, less than forty years after the two services from GWR and L&SWR first opened, the Stacey family suffered a terrible loss.

The two platforms at Salisbury Station were divided by a simple screen that separated the trains of the two companies. Unbelievably, both ran their first train of the day at exactly the same time and it meant anyone working on the line ahead needed to watch out for not one but two engines building up a head of steam.

Father and son, Charles and Frank Stacey, worked as packers, repairing broken rails, usually just outside the main station before the track became a single line. On 6 November, they heard the L&SWR train approaching first, the quicker of the two to leave the platform. Yet, instead of moving to the side of the track, they simply stepped onto the other line, their backs towards the oncoming GWR engine!

The impact was horrific. Both men were carried several yards along the track and fell beneath the wheels. Charles was instantly beheaded while Frank was savagely disembowelled.

It had been an accident waiting to happen. The inquest blamed two trains approaching at the same time, one masking the noise of the other. But it also highlighted the sharp left-hand curve in the line outside the station – the one which twenty-six years later would witness the worst crash in history – which meant drivers leaving the station could see someone on the line only when it was too late to pull up. That both men were from the same family made the tragedy even more distressing.

―∞∞―

recovered from beneath the twisted, mangled wreckage.

The victims

Nearly all of the victims were American, save for the crew of the three trains. Many were returned home to the United States for burial, their bodies embalmed ahead of the long journey by sea. One Canadian visitor, Reverend King, once a native of Plymouth, was buried at Fisherton. Thousands emerged onto the streets as his cortege made its mournful way along Fisherton Street towards the cathedral and back for his interment. Businesses put up black shutters or drew down blinds and Salisbury's mayor joined the official mourners, the mace of office draped in black crepe.

All the following week, school trips, concerts and outings were cancelled out of respect.

One of the saddest tragedies involved a young couple who had travelled on their honeymoon. The bride survived but her new husband was much less fortunate. She returned with his corpse on board the North German liner, *Kaiser Wilhelm II*, as did many others, dead and survivors alike. Others returned on board the *Teutonic*, bound from Liverpool. Perhaps the most harrowing story involved the gentleman travelling with his wife and children. He had survived the crash but had spent many long, interminable minutes penned inside their private compartment, his dead family around him.

The cause

As the clearing up reached its conclusion, one question was being asked: the accident had undoubtedly happened as the train travelled into the curve much too quickly, but why had it been running so fast?

Almost from the beginning, Salisbury had been served by two separate rail companies – GWR and L&SWR. They used separate lines in and out of the station and there had been strenuous competition to complete the journey from Plymouth to London in the shortest possible time. Record speeds were being achieved. The driver of the boat train, William Robins, had been an experienced railwayman and it was ascertained that if he was behind schedule it was not by any great amount, but it was true that he had never before driven a boat train, or passed non-stop through Salisbury Station. The train hit the curve at 60–70mph (the limit was 30mph). The allegations that the thrill-seeking American passengers had tipped the crew to go as fast as they could were rejected.

Two controversial theories were put forward. Firstly, that the crew had been overcome by carbon monoxide escaping from the poorly made furnace – other similar accidents had occurred under similarly unexplained circumstances. The second idea gained more support. The accident, in which nearly thirty people suffered horrendous deaths, was due to the fierce competition that existed between the rival train companies. It had happened on the day before GWR were due to launch their new, quicker service between Berkshire and Hampshire; and it had not been long since one of their drivers had allegedly reached 100mph on another line. Had Robins strived to send a personal message of defiance to the progressive GWR on behalf of his beloved, but slower, L&SWR? Had, in fact, a lust for supremacy led him to hit Salisbury Station at more than twice the legal limit, a decision that would end in such tragic loss of life? With both himself and his fireman killed, and decades before the invention of the data-recording black box, we shall never know.

AD 1888

JACK THE RIPPER COMES TO SALISBURY!

'Royal Suspect Kept in Local Mad House'

OVER TEN LONG weeks in 1888, the notorious Whitechapel murderer, Jack the Ripper, viciously slaughtered five victims by butchering and mutilating their poor bodies until his unexplained bloodlust was inexplicably satisfied. Some commentators have since argued that there may have been another reason for the sudden end to his killing ...

At the time of the murders, Fisherton House Lunatic Asylum, on the Wilton Road north of Salisbury, was one of the most celebrated criminal lunatic asylums in the country. Housed here were numerous killers, many infamous and most, if not all, deemed too mad to be tried and hanged as responsible agents. Amidst rife speculation about Jack the Ripper's true identity, the queen's grandson and second in line to the throne of England, Prince Albert Victor, Duke of Clarence and Avondale, became a chief suspect. Just as those scurrilous rumours were never truly silenced, claims of his subsequent incarceration at Fisherton House have similarly refused to die.

On 8 November 1888, the Ripper's winter of terror ended, but not before his worst crime to date. Mary Kelly was a 24-year-old prostitute, working in one of the dark alleys that were rife in Victorian London. That night, she met the man who would become her killer. Having agreed a price, she led him back to her nearby room and the world would never know such horror again.

Unlike his previous murders, the Ripper carried out his violent attack in the relative safety of behind closed doors, giving him time to go much further than he had done before. Mary's body – or, rather, what was left of it – was discovered the next morning by the rent collector who, peering inquisitively through the grimy window, reeled backwards and spilt the contents of his stomach onto the grubby pavement. The girl's body, pathetically laid out on the single bed, had been entirely dismembered.

The police find a victim. (Illustrated Police News)

Official photographs taken at the time show the true horror of the crime. Her heart lay on the pillow alongside the head, her other organs, including the uterus, scattered around the room like grotesque ornaments.

Following that gruesome episode, nothing more was ever heard of the Ripper. He – or she – had simply stopped killing; or perhaps, more likely, they had been forced to stop; for example, through incarceration. It was and remains an extraordinary finale to the serial killings. Was the Ripper banged up in Fisherton House to protect the world from him and himself from the world?

At Fisherton House in 1880, despite tight security and forcefully silenced tongues, allegations of Prince Albert Victor's arrival began to leak through its wrought iron gates, into the public's imagination and on to the pages of a gratuitous press. Though never proved at the time, many felt there could be no smoke without fire. But, if true, then no patient at Fisherton House would ever be more famous than him.

The earliest rumours that the prince was Jack the Ripper were easily accepted. He was a drinker, womaniser and gambler, and was frequently reported across the newspapers with tales of battles against his personal demons. A clairvoyant, R.J. Lees, also claimed at the time of the killings that he had visualised the royal figure carrying out his crimes before they happened.

The young prince was also denounced by Dalton and Stephen as an atrocious pupil, disinterested in learning and averse to doing anything useful. He had been considered weak from birth until his premature (and, for the authorities, convenient) death. As a child, he had suffered from typhoid fever and was treated by Sir William Gull, Royal Physician.

As an adult, he got caught up in the Cleveland Street scandal, when a male brothel used by (then illicit) homosexuals was raided by the police. The future king was rumoured to have been a client but was whisked away from further damaging publicity. A few months later,

SO MANY SUSPECTS

There are more people suspected of being Jack the Ripper than there were ever victims – thankfully! As well as the prince and Sir William Gull, Lees the clairvoyant was suspected; the Shakespearean actor, Richard Mansfield, who at the time shocked London audiences with his on-stage transmutation from Dr Jekyll into Mr Hyde; and a Polish barber and philanderer whose name was one of the first given to police. Other names and theories have included a foreign agent, sent to England to bring its forces of law and order to its knees; a German sailor with an insatiable desire to mutilate; and even Lewis Carroll – not the first time his name has appeared in this book. At last, one theorist put forward a case for Jack the Ripper to be renamed Jacqueline the Ripper – that the evil butcher of Whitechapel was, in fact, a woman. The case continues … will it ever be solved? Has it in fact been solved without the proof to make it an irrefutable theory?

an American woman alleged that he was the father of her illegitimate child, a son who subsequently tried to blackmail George V (the prince's brother) by claiming the king was his uncle. Finally, more pertinent perhaps, Albert Victor was accused of contracting syphilis, a disease known to cause insanity. But could it have driven him mad enough to butcher so many women with such unbridled ferocity?

How soon talk at Buckingham Palace and Whitehall turned to what must be done with the errant prince will now surely never be known. However, he is believed to have been forcibly removed to Fisherton sometime after Mary Kelly's death. He was 'officially' certified insane by Sir William Gull; but was he protecting himself? Gull had become a chief suspect in the hunt for the Ripper; had the prince witnessed the killer at work, been perhaps his apprentice or confidante? Or was 'Jack' really Reverend Dalton, the prince's childhood tutor? Or James Kenneth Stephen, another tutor, who from the day Albert Victor died on 14 January 1892, starved himself to death by refusing food for the next twenty days? After all, he had been suffering from psychosis since receiving a brain injury two years before the killings.

Fisherton's connection to Jack the Ripper slowly dissipated until 1970 when Thomas Stowell, a Southampton doctor, made his astonishing claim. With mystery and enigma worthy of a royal cover-up, he wrote in the November issue of the *Criminologist* magazine claiming that he had concealed papers for fifty years which clearly showed

A portrait of the prince, and possibly Jack the Ripper. (THP)

the prince's involvement in the killer's reign. On 2 November, he appeared on television, apparently 'confirming' his belief that Albert Victor was indeed Jack the Ripper. This time, the national press, including *The Times*, went to town.

On 5 November, Stowell wrote a letter to the erstwhile publication, stating that he had made no direct association with the late prince, a self-contradiction that the paper duly printed the following Monday, the 9th. But by then, Dr Stowell was dead.

In a further twist, Stowell's son announced that he had burnt his father's papers over the weekend. He had no interest in the case, he announced testily, and had 'read just sufficient to make certain there was nothing of importance' in the relevant folders!

So the prince, the Ripper and Fisherton House took their secrets to the grave ...

AD 1910–1911

THE CARD CHEAT WITH A BAD HAND

Dismemberment and Clandestine Whores!

THE HAUNCH OF Venison, a fourteenth-century inn in Minster Street (so-called for 700 years), possesses possibly one of the city's most unusual and ghastly relics. During renovation in 1910–11, workmen removed what they thought was just another piece of plain panelling yet what lay behind sent them scurrying for the door. Coated in dust and placed seemingly with deliberation, was a withered human hand. Its fingers bony and elongated, had evidently remained undisturbed for many years, for in its cadaverous grasp were a number of playing cards, quite regular and plain but incredibly old.

Frightening indeed, but how and why had the hand been put there? Why, indeed, was it found without a body to go with it? There were just two possibilities: either it was a 'glory hand' or a cheat who had been brutally punished (judging from the way it grasped the cards).

So what of the first suggestion? 'Glory hands' were trophies, thought to bring good luck or protection from evil spirits. They were the preserved appendages of hanged criminals, often the left hand (attributed to the Devil) or, in the case of murderers, the hand they used to kill

their victim. Their original use is now shrouded in doubt, but popular folklore recommended placing a candle made from the fat of the person whose hand it was into his morbid grasp – that is, for the hand to hold a candle made from the same flesh. As well as burning eternally, it was believed such a candle could open any locked door the carrier encountered or provide the user with supernatural powers, such as rendering anyone they meet motionless (*see* text box).

The other explanation for the existence of the strange artefact has proved more popular. The severed hand is thought to have been cut from a card shark in some dim and distant age. It is believed that the extremity's one-time owner cheated his cohorts at whist, a card game popular since at least the eighteenth century. Somewhat vexed by his deception, one of the gang drew a blade, pinned the cheat's arm to the table and sliced off the cheat's hand. Then, judging by where the hand was found, tossed the severed limb onto the fire! The putrid stench of burning flesh must have filled the air as a now utterly remorseful cheat grasped the ragged stump of his arm and tried to staunch the profuse flow of blood.

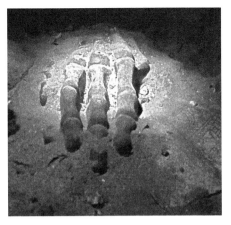

The skeleton hand. (Courtesy of The Haunch Of Venison, Salisbury)

The hand today fittingly resides where it was found, though in the past it has twice been stolen. The first time was in 2004 when the hand was on open display. Perhaps the thief experienced ill fortune from the hand, which, of course, is said to be cursed, and it was mysteriously returned six weeks later.

The landlord of the pub sensibly thereafter kept the hand secure behind a glass-fronted grille, going so far as to fit tight screws and a strong padlock. Yet this too proved no deterrent to yet another intrepid collector. Armed presumably with a screwdriver and a strong constitution, he or she removed the hand, furtively leaving the inn with their famous trophy – some time later the grim relic was returned once again!

The Haunch of Venison has its rightful place in Salisbury's darker history, but not only for its withered hand. In a time long forgotten, the local church had its dealings with the inn, where the cathedral clerics held meetings and even services in the upper rooms that today bear names reflecting that past association. Perhaps in recognition of such clerical patronage,

GLORY HANDS

Legends about the uses of glory hands are legion – and spurious. Yet if interpretations are correct, several of these macabre relics do exist. One of the more famous anecdotes involves an attempted robbery at an isolated tavern where a rough-looking vagrant had just been granted shelter for the night. With the family in bed and believing himself alone, the ungrateful wretch pulled out the glory hand he carried and placed it on a table in the bar. Rubbing the five fingernails with a rag, he struck a match and set each one in turn alight. Only one of them would not catch.

Nevertheless, knowing that each lit finger meant the inhabitants of the house would remain fast asleep for as long as the flames burned, he believed he was safe from detection. However, one of the servants was wide awake and, worse, watched him as he went about his illicit business. Eventually, she was able to lock the thief in a separate room while she attempted to rouse the landlord and his family. Unsuccessful, she returned to the glory hand and tried blowing out the flames, again without success. Beer poured over it didn't work, neither did water. At last, she tried a jug of milk and the flames died. Needless to say, the family woke up instantly and the servant led them to the burglar in his impromptu prison. Tonight, his helping hand had let him down.

when the cloisters at the cathedral were renovated, the intricate tile floor was carefully lifted and re-laid in the public bar of the inn.

Even more colourfully, it is possible that past members of the church may have regularly veered from the path of righteousness whilst visiting the pub – led astray by wine, song and women. Rumours abound that a secret tunnel connecting the public house with the thirteenth-century St Thomas' church, still standing, was used by the clergy to pass unseen into the inn when it was reputedly used as the local and allegedly very popular brothel!

It would be nice to think that such anti-clerical behaviour led to the renowned fifteenth-century Doom painting of the Last Judgment, which still adorns the chancel arch of St Thomas. Believed to be the largest of its kind in England, it was (almost disappointingly) created in recognition of a pilgrim's safe return.

AD 1912
DEATH IN SERVICE

The First Military Air Fatalities

WITH THE DAWN of flying came the advent of air crashes. At Airman's Cross, to the north of Salisbury, a monument to the memory of two unfortunate pilots stands proudly as a Listed Building. It was moved recently as part of the impressive new Stonehenge Visitor Centre but was retained – such is its continued importance in the annals of military fatalities.

On 5 July 1912, Captain Eustace Broke Loraine and Staff Sergeant Richard Wilson died in the first ever air crash to involve men on active service, as they performed a routine flight over the Stonehenge encampment. At about 5.30 a.m., the pair took off from Larkhill with Loraine at the helm. Reaching an altitude of 400ft, the Nieuport plane rattled alarmingly, then flipped right over before careering to the ground. Wilson died instantly, but Loraine lived on for a few brief moments, reaching Bulford Military Hospital alive but unconscious before he too sadly passed away. It is unclear to this day exactly what happened to the wreckage; archaeological investigations have failed to recover its remains and its exact location is still uncertain.

However, in the immediate aftermath, the site became something of a macabre hunting ground for ghoulish souvenir hunters. A photograph shows what appears to be a Sunday trip out to the crash site, with overalled men combing the wreck while ladies in fine dresses enjoy a picnic, complete with hamper and blanket!

The funerals of both men took place with full military honours, followed by hundreds of onlookers deeply moved by the tragedy. Wilson, just 29, was buried in Andover, his gun-carriage bier conveyed along the town's closed roads and accompanied by representatives of every military unit then serving on Salisbury Plain. Loraine, 33 and a

Captain Loraine's funeral procession.
(Author's collection)

Grahame White's Nieuport Monoplane. (LC-DIG-ggbain-09564)

veteran of the South African War, was taken from Bulford Camp under full military honours to the rail station, attended by every officer as well as several complete companies, squadrons and a military band. He travelled by train to his home near Ipswich from where, two days later, he was conveyed to the local church amidst one of the largest military funerals ever to have taken place. He was laid to rest with his pioneering reputation secured in military folklore.

Both men died heroes – the first of the infant Royal Flying Corps to be killed on active service.

Despite the rarity of the crash in military terms, Wilson and Loraine were astonishingly (yet in other ways unsurprisingly) the 158th and 159th fatalities since aviation began. Many more would follow. On 17 July 1913, Major Alexander Hewetson was practice-flying over Larkhill in preparation for his pilot's license.

All was fine until his Bristol monoplane veered into a sidespin and plummeted to the ground, killing him instantly. The Secretary of State for War, speaking in the House of Commons, quickly pointed out that the major had no connection with the Royal Flying Corps and had not been on RFC business when the accident happened. Indeed, Major Hewetson, an Irishman by birth and presently on leave from the Royal Artillery in India, was using up some holiday. At the inquest, held on the day of the crash, it was accepted that it had arisen purely from human error. That is, Major Hewetson had attempted to turn the plane but banked too sharply, sending the machine into its dive.

The coroner asked a witness, Mr Jullerot, whether he thought 44, the major's age, was 'rather late in life to begin flying'? The witness replied that he had thought it best for men of that advanced age not to take up the pastime at all! The jury decided there was no culpable negligence on anyone's part and advised a verdict of 'accidental death'.

DAWN OF POWERED FLIGHT – SAMUEL F. CODY

In America, the pioneers of sustainable flight had been the Wright brothers and in England it was Samuel F. Cody. On 16 October 1908, he was the first person in Britain to make a continuous flight of a powered, 'heavier than air' machine; flying his self-designed and self-built aircraft for 1,400ft at an altitude of 18ft before crash-landing into trees. The aviation history of Britain had begun.

Cody had been taken on by the British Army to design, build and test new planes, but he was dismissed after the army decided there was no future in flight! However, in 1912, with flying firmly back on the agenda, the Military Air Trials were held on Salisbury Plain where Cody had hoped to enter either of his two machines. Both though had been wrecked in recent crashes – one hitting and killing a cow on impact. (The colourful Cody lost the subsequent damages case in which he suggested that the cow had been suicidal!) Undeterred, he built a third plane from the surviving bits of the ruined pair – a sort of aeronautical 'ringer' – and went on to win the trials.

But on 7 August 1913, Cody's luck ran out. A test flight 300ft from the ground ended in tragedy when he and his passenger fell to their deaths when the plane literally disintegrated around them. He was buried with full military honours and his funeral was attended by some 100,000 people. His statue in Farnborough, where he did most of his flying, was unveiled on 7 August 2013 – 100 years to the day of his untimely death.

A monument survives at Fargo Plantation, east of Airman's Cross.

As flying became more popular, so the death toll kept rising. In November 1917, Captain Deuchar of the delightfully named Northern Cyclists Battalion, was attached to the Royal Flying Corps. Spending time practising his flying, his plane was seen over the centre of Salisbury moments before it entered a spin and nosedived into a field close to Old Sarum. One Mrs Blades witnessed the appalling accident and immediately ran to help. Thrashing through a hedge, her progress was halted as an explosion tore apart the plane, the flames and smoke temporarily blinding her sight.

More help soon arrived and, with the smoke clearing but the fire still well alight, she raced toward the cockpit. A ghastly sight awaited her. As she approached Deuchar, the poor man lifted his head and looked straight at her. She and others tried desperately to release him, but all too quickly – yet mercifully – he died.

By this time, aircraft were fitted with safety harnesses to stop the pilot being thrown clear in the event of crashes, but were fitted with a quick-release mechanism for obvious reasons. It was considered likely that Captain Deuchar, whilst dying of shock and burns, had been trapped not by his harness but by the wreckage itself.

Not all fatalities came from being suspended in the air – on occasion being on the ground was just as dangerous. In 1912 (evidently a bad year for such things), Leonard Williams, a 15-year-old Amesbury boy, died close by the hangars at Larkhill from a broken skull and three crushed vertebrae after a plane being flown on a routine training exercise landed safely – but then carried on into a crowd of about 150 onlookers.

Lieutenant Ashton, the pilot, had landed the Bristol Tractor Biplane about 150 yards from the sheds as usual. But a light wind had pushed the aircraft along the ground, causing it to gather speed as it headed straight for the spectators. Foolishly, some of them had already come alongside the plane and, in the confusion, the machine flipped into the air, doing a complete somersault and trapping poor Williams beneath the resultant wreckage.

There were other casualties: a 17-year-old youth with a badly injured head and back; a young man with a broken collarbone; and numerous members of the now-scattered crowd suffering cuts and bruises. In the panic, some had managed to lie prone on the grass and allow the plane to pass over them!

At the inquest the coroner, addressing the flying school manager, asked:

'I take it from you that you have no control over the crowd at all when you are practising?'

'None whatever.'

'Don't you think you had better try and get it?' he responded pithily.

'We have done our best, sir by getting mounted police when the Air Corps are practicing ...'

The gaps in health and safety notwithstanding, the coroner, in summing up towards a verdict of 'accidental death', added that whether there was any negligence or not, it must have been slight and not culpable. The jury should therefore take no notice of it!

AD 1913

YOU CAN'T CHOOSE YOUR FAMILY

The Tragic Case of Dorothy Jefferies

JUST BEFORE 3 P.M. on Saturday 24 May 1913, Frederick Jefferies, a local bookseller, newsagent and much-respected family man of Castle Street, staggered into the city police station and declared: 'I want to give myself up. I have been and killed my little girl. I did it with a razor.' Police Constable Eyres, listening with horror, ran through to the telephone office at the back of the building and pleaded with Sergeant William Cutler to return with him to the front desk.

The senior policeman had known Jefferies for more than a decade and he could scarcely believe what his constable was telling him as they neared the lobby. When he saw his old friend, struggling to stand, his breathing shallow and rapid and his clothes, hands and boots all covered in blood, his heart sank.

'Where is she, Frederick?'

'In the bedroom, on the bed.' He could barely speak the words.

Instructing Eyres to remain with Jefferies, Cutler roused Dr Armitage, Assistant Divisional Police Surgeon, and raced round to Castle Street, to the home and premises of the family he thought he had known so well. They were there in minutes. As they entered the busy shop,

a small bell tinkled against the opening door and Annie Jefferies, Frederick's wife, looked up from behind the counter.

'William, you look troubled. Whatever's the matter?'

Cutler couldn't believe his ears. She was either ignorant of what Jefferies had related or he had lied. Not answering, he led Dr Armitage upstairs, walking through the small sitting room to the bedroom. On a chair lay a discarded blood-soaked towel.

Cutler pushed open the door. Unable to stop the fraught woman from rushing

Frederick Jefferies. (Courtesy of the Wiltshire and Swindon History Centre)

past, he saw a stomach-turning scene of carnage, with little Dorothy Jefferies lying limp at its centre. Her body was indeed on the bed, positioned as though she had fallen asleep. The large amount of blood soaking the counterpane and gathering on the floor, however, revealed the grimmer truth.

Armitage went immediately to the child. A woollen muffler had been tied tightly at the back of her neck, covering her mouth but leaving her throat exposed. The flesh was sliced through from left to right – she had died instantly, at least. Cutler noted that the pool of blood contained footprints and the doctor confirmed, from the nature of the wound and the way the blood had formed both on and beside the bed, that the poor girl had been attacked from behind whilst standing. It was not reported who first saw the razor, but the bloodstained weapon was found lying close by, the rest of a full shaving kit spread out on the dressing table, as though abandoned in use.

Sealing the crime scene from prying eyes, Cutler and Armitage returned to the station, the visit having taken less than fifty minutes from when Jefferies had first entered the police station. It would take a lot longer to get to the bottom of this appalling case.

The police sergeant wasted no time in charging Jefferies with the murder of his own daughter, Dorothy Madeline, 9 years old and widely acknowledged to have been his favourite.

Dorothy Jefferies. (Courtesy of the Wiltshire and Swindon History Centre)

outside the council chambers though Jefferies, by an act of charity, had been taken there in advance of the usual start time, when the streets outside were still quiet. Annie Jefferies, dressed all in black, attended with her family, but struggled to remain conscious as her husband was brought to the dock.

The chief constable led the prosecution, taking time only to examine his sergeant, Cutler, before he requested an adjournment to the following week. Rumours and conjecture about Jefferies' long-term mental state had already surfaced and the senior officer wanted more time to investigate their veracity.

Police court

The hearing in front of the Salisbury magistrates took place on Monday morning. A large crowd had gathered

Coroner's inquest

That same evening, the coroner, Mr Buchanan Smith, held his inquest, also in the council chambers. Only he, his assistants, the witnesses and jury were allowed inside.

Smith instantly reminded the jury that they were here only to discern the cause of death; and, if they felt they could identify a human agent, to name them. They could not – and he was adamant – comment on the named person's circumstances, particularly his or her state of mind.

Dorothy's body was identified by her uncle, local butcher James Millard, while Mr Jackson, Jefferies' solicitor, acknowledged the coroner's instructions and assured the jury that more could and would be said during the course of the inevitable trial.

Trial, circumstantial evidence and verdict

Frederick Jefferies was brought back before the magistrates on 2 June and committed to trial at the County Assizes in Devizes on 13 October. Evidence about his mental health was presented in detail: Jackson had stuck to his word. Jefferies' family had an alarming history of mental illness. Two of his aunts and a great uncle had been, or were still, detained in various county asylums; an uncle (subsequently declared insane) had hanged himself; his mother's cousin (also declared insane) had put a gun against his head and pulled the trigger; and Frederick's

own cousin had poisoned himself, the coroner's jury finding him insane at the time of the act.

With such a family history, Jefferies' trial tried to identify the 'blue-touch-paper' that had triggered a loving, devoted father to brutally murder his own daughter. It was decided that the recent death of Jefferies' mother – who had lived with them at Castle Street – tipped him over the edge, having left him so distraught that he had begged his brother to stay with them in the house. Frederick Jefferies was found guilty of murder but pardoned on the grounds of insanity and detained at His Majesty's pleasure in a hospital for the criminally insane.

Funeral

Dorothy Jefferies was taken on her last journey in a glass carriage, a polished elm coffin surrounded by floral tributes. A nickel nameplate simply read:

DOROTHY MADELINE JEFFERIES
– DIED MAY 24TH 1913 – AGED 9
YEARS

Two more carriages followed, conveying her distraught family, while the undertakers and two policemen led the cortege to the church. The ceremony was short, but their pain would last a lifetime.

AD 1914–1918
BLOODY WAR

Salisbury: Gateway to Horror

THE HORRORS OF the Great War were felt more keenly in Salisbury and its Plain to the north. Here, thousands of troops, regular and conscripted, were introduced to army life, before being sent to the killing fields of the Western Front. Throughout the entire wretched conflict, preparations for war were endured by those who passed through the camps, fields and billets on Salisbury Plain.

Preparing for war

There are still signs of the training men of all nationalities undertook before leaving the safety of home shores. A network of zigzag lines still punctures the great Plain, like sharp-edged vipers with a bite to match. For these are practice trenches, dug out by new recruits as they prepared for that horrific First World War experience – trench warfare.

Some survive today as earthworks, visible on aerial photographs, often relics of a specific nation's or regiment's introduction to these hellish homes from home – complete with temporary stores, medicine posts and latrines. The skills and proficiency learnt on the Plain were put to use on the Western Front and led to the survival (temporary, at least) of hundreds if not thousands of men. Of course, for many, they contributed instead to their deaths, amidst the mud, guts and bullets that signified early twentieth-century trench warfare.

Going to war

Many of the men who saw action in wartime France began their army careers in Salisbury, at one of the numerous camps on the Plain. One of the most reputed, Bulford, was originally devised ahead of the second Boer War. Officially 'opened for business' from 1900, it received thousands of new recruits, from the Pals regiments, conscripts, volunteers – people like Arthur Powell, my own great uncle, who enlisted with the Royal Field Artillery and who died at Arras in 1918 (*see* text box).

Men like him were sent here ahead of their own personal journeys into hell. Passing through tents, wooden huts, temporary billets (all with their own unique aromas and sounds) bulling boots, perfecting gun drill, always under orders of the regular soldiers and the senior NCOs. The excitement of the early years of war, when volunteers prepared for their part in a conflict sure to be 'over

Corner of the battlefield near Arras.
(LC-DIG-det-4a25883)

by Christmas', was quickly replaced with an intense fear. With it, sometimes because of it, tragic deaths occurred even before they had left the camp.

The rise in suicides was devastating; self-inflicted gunshot wounds and even drowning were among the most common modus. William Williams, originally from North Wales, was found floating in the River Avon at Stratford-sub-Castle a month after going missing. He had already served on the front but had returned to camp, suffering from shell shock and debilitating night terrors. An unnamed man, aged 25, shot himself in the head after seeing his close friend posted overseas, knowing he was very likely to be killed. He opted to join his pal on 'the other side'.

Other fatalities were pure accidents. In 1915, with the war just months old, William Shannon of the Scots Fusiliers was training with his regiment on the nature of explosive material and stood up at precisely the wrong time during a demonstration of exploding gun-cotton. He died instantly, a rogue projectile penetrating his skull and lacerating the brain; though his officer

in charge believed he had only fainted at the report.

In 1916, in one of the badly lit huts at Larkhill Camp, Charles Sargentson, an Australian soldier, died from a vicious wound to the stomach while 'larking about' with bayonets and guns. His unwitting killer had not seen him remove the sheath of the blade moments before he lunged forward in mock assault. A year later, Harold Andreassen, also Australian and just 24, died at Rollestone Camp while practising with a Lewis machine gun. His hand was almost severed from his arm and his right collarbone was 'holed' by the cartridge. The inquest found that a live round had become mixed up with the dummies.

In 1918, a young soldier kicked at something on the ground which turned out to be a 16lb bomb. It exploded instantly, killing both him and his comrade beside him. They had a combined age of 35. Ten days later, the war was over.

Returning from war

For those brought home early, it usually meant suffering from the worst kinds of injury, both physical and mental. Treated initially in the field and subsequently in one of the front-line medical centres, the most seriously hurt were brought back to Britain to the military hospitals, such as those on Salisbury Plain. Here they could receive specialist treatment and much-needed convalescence.

These military hospitals, like Bulford and the new one at Fargo – erected specifically for the war – treated some of the most bloodied and battered. The exponential increase in the number of casualties of war was overwhelming and Fargo, with over 1,000 beds and accommodation for the nursing staff, arguably became one of the largest and busiest British military hospitals ever known.

When we talk of military hospitals, we generally think of the human cost of war. But there were four-legged casualties too, and, in particular, the horses of the Great War. On the front, 500,000 died serving with the British. The Horse Isolation Hospital may not be as well known as its human equivalents at Bulford and Fargo, and its history is much forgotten, but it will hopefully soon re-emerge through renewed investigation. Its existence on the Plain marks out the war in its total cost – men, women and animals alike.

Mobilising for war

The development of light railways made the movement of troops and goods between military camps much easier. The Amesbury & Military Camp Light Railway (AMCLR), constructed before the war, linked Amesbury to Bulford Camp. As soon as Britain was drawn in, additional lines were laid out for operational necessity. The first extension ran to Larkhill Military Camp, while a second one went further, to Rollestone Camp (the site of a balloon school in the early years of military aviation); then continuing on to the new military hospital at Fargo and finally dividing to Druid's Lodge in the south-west and the Stonehenge hangars to the east. With so much movement across the Plain, accidents were inevitable ...

Much of the AMCLR was operated by the Royal Engineers and, just after

A First World War Howitzer. (Library of Congress LC-DIG-ds-00226)

Christmas 1917, one of their company met with a particularly unpleasant death after finishing work near Countess Crossing. Waiting for the train from Ratfyn to Larkhill Camp to travel past, he set off across the single line not noticing a second train reversing in his direction, coming to assist another which had broken down further along. The 56-year-old engineer met his end in gruesome fashion as one of his legs was completely severed, the other almost so and his head gravely injured after colliding with the train.

Remembering war

Every year, we gather to pay our respects and to remember the dead – as well as those whom death left behind. Many who died at Fargo Military Hospital were interred at the Tidworth Military Cemetery. Other casualties of the war can be found amongst civilian cemeteries and churchyards; including Devizes Road and London Road cemeteries in Salisbury; and outside, at Alderbury, Bemerton, Durrington, East Harnham, Rollestone, West Harnham, Wilton – the list goes on.

No community escaped the heart-rending sorrow and tragedy of the Great War. Salisbury was no exception.

ARTHUR POWELL MM

Arthur Powell qualified for call-up on 15 July 1915, joining 71st Brigade Royal Field Artillery at Bulford Camp. Travelling to Southampton on the Military Light Railway and the main line from Amesbury, he set foot on French soil for his first overseas trip. Driver Powell, 25182, was attached to RFA Headquarters at the outrageously named Quality Street and, in October 1916, was awarded the Military Medal. Two years later, he became a Medical Orderly with the RAMC (Royal Army Medical Corps) and tended hundreds of injured comrades, saving many who would otherwise have perished. In recognition of his qualities and talents, he was promoted to bombardier.

Arthur Powell. (Author's collection)

In March 1918, eight months before the end of the 'war to end all wars', Arthur and 71st Brigade were attached to 15th (Scottish) Division, part of the Third Army fighting to repel what the enemy thought would be their greatest and decisive battle. On 28 March, in the First Battle of Arras (of 1918), the Allies were made to withdraw, as a prelude to their successful final push and Germany's total surrender.

As enemy shelling reached fever pitch, the retreating forces suffered heavy casualties. Ignoring all danger, Arthur Powell went out into no-man's-land to help the wounded. One was a young gunner, serving under 'one of the brilliant young soldiers of the war, Major Graham of 'C' Battery', who stood bravely by as enemy fire continued to rain down. When a shell landed within yards of the small group, all three were killed instantly. It was later reported that Arthur had not suffered and simply looked surprised.

His last written words, revealing both the horror and naïve optimism in war, came in a letter to his mother begun on 20 March 1918:

> Dearest Mother, I hope he [his younger brother, George] will never come out here again … I will not be sorry when this lot is over but still I do not think it will last long now … I started to write this letter 4 days ago, but owing to certain things, I was not able to finish it till now, Love to all.

The note was dated 24 March.

Four days later, like so many before him, Arthur Powell was buried where he fell. His former comrades erected a cross to mark the spot and, at the end of the war, a massive effort was made to locate the fallen and to give them formal graves. Arthur's body was exhumed and reinterred at Feuchy Chapel Cemetery, Wancourt near Arras. Like them all, he will never be forgotten.

His association with Salisbury, no matter how brief, remains special to his family and especially to the present author.

THE MURDEROUS, MONOCLED MUTINEER

The Life and 'Crimes' of Percy Toplis

PERCY TOPLIS' ASSOCIA-TIONS with Salisbury originated not only from his time at Bulford army camp, but sadly from his alleged murder of local taxi driver, Sidney Spicer. This brutal act triggered a manhunt the likes of which Britain had not seen for many years, for Toplis was not just a murderer, he was also the famed Monocled Mutineer – army deserter, rebel, thief, womaniser, impersonator and alleged leader of the British Army mutiny at Etaples, northern France. Toplis was a colourful character with a mono-chrome view of right and wrong and he was hailed a hero and a villain in equal measure. This is the story of his final days, beginning with the murder which *The Salisbury Times and South Wilts Gazette* referred to as 'The Motor Car Tragedy'.

On 24 April 1920, Percy Toplis hid behind a hedge on the main Salisbury–Amesbury road. As the taxi approached, it stopped and its driver, 29-year-old Spicer, stepped out and lifted a jerrycan of petrol out of the boot. As he stood filling the empty tank, Toplis came out of his hiding place and moved up behind: 'I need you to take me to Andover.'

Spicer wheeled around. 'I can't, I've got a fare to Bulford.' He nodded to the passengers inside the car. 'I can pick you up you on the way back if you like.'

Toplis reluctantly agreed and walked off in the direction of the Hampshire town.

The next day, Sidney Spicer was found shot in the head, his body dumped on the roadside at a lonely spot on Thruxton Down. From the nature of his wound – the bullet was still lodged in his skull – he had been shot from behind, possibly by a passenger sitting in the rear seat of his taxi. The murder weapon – a revolver – had been held horizontally as his killer squeezed the trigger. Cash, driving license and gold watch were all missing, as was the vehicle.

Within hours, Percy Toplis was Britain's most-wanted and, by the establishment at least, most-hated man. He was debonair, rakish, ostentatious – a cad – and a soldier, a protestor, a liar, a deserter. On one occasion, he had abandoned his comrades at the front by claiming compassionate leave after the sudden death of his wife during childbirth. Only he had no wife; and there was no child! Yet he returned home to a hero's welcome, tying a bandage around his knee to feign an injury that had brought him home. At the same

Victim Sidney Spicer. (Courtesy of the Wiltshire and Swindon History Centre)

time, he adopted one of his favourite disguises, of an army officer (he was in fact a private) and returned home to Chesterfield a hero, victim and prodigal son. His picture was displayed proudly in one of the shops on the high street.

But in the late spring/early summer of 1920, he was a suspected murderer. The photograph was presented to the police to use as a wanted poster.

Over the years, Toplis had acquired a wardrobe of officers' uniforms which he donned with bare-faced regularity; often to impress the ladies, frequently to gain entry into the upper echelons of society and even gaining dinner in the officers' mess at Bulford while he was on the run as a deserter! His iconic accessory was his gold monocle, which gave him an air of confidence and superiority. He bought it in Bristol for £15 and it was still in his pocket the day he died. That day was getting closer.

Back in Salisbury, the murder of Sidney Spicer had made Britain as unsafe for Toplis as had been the Western Front. Yet his bravado knew no limits. He returned to Bulford Camp, claiming to be attached to another regiment, the RAF! On the evening of 24 April, he made

contact with his old friend, Private Harry Fallows, offering the young man a lift to Swansea. They set off later that night, almost certainly in Spicer's taxi (it was later found abandoned in the city), and the two men were soon under suspicion for murder.

Toplis' behaviour on the bizarre road trip was erratic. On their way south, he burned his 'spare clothes' in Savernake Forest and, on their arrival in Wales, insisted on swapping hats with Fallows, then disappeared for clandestine meetings with 'friends', only to return saying he had sold the car. Toplis eventually bought Fallows a train ticket back to Bulford and the Murderous Monocled Mutineer went on the run alone.

He was found guilty in absentia for Sidney Spicer's death, largely on Fallows' evidence. Police made a connection between Toplis and the unfortunate taxi driver involving a fuel scam, in which petrol from Bulford Camp was siphoned off and sold on the black market, in particular to the local taxi firms. Spicer had allegedly been part of it and had threatened to expose Toplis if the 'going rate' per gallon was not lowered.

Penrith in Cumberland is 300 miles from Salisbury. By the time Toplis arrived, he had left a trail of death and devastation in Salisbury, Swansea, Edinburgh, Chepstow, Cirencester, Banffshire, Penrith and, if reports were to be believed, up to 100 other places across the British Isles! On 6 June, after six weeks on the run, Toplis' luck finally ran out.

A local police constable, Alfred Fulton, came upon Toplis as he made his way from Carlisle to Penrith.

MUTINY IN THE BULL RING

———— ⟨⟩ ————

In 1917, Toplis had his most famous – and debated – episode of a brief, eventful army life. The British training camp for new conscripts was based in northern France: the 'Bull Ring' at Etaples. He had reportedly deserted months before, joining hundreds of comrades in a network of underground camps and tunnels. From here he allegedly led the greatest rebellion the British Army had ever known (and was desperate to cover up), against the harsh regime and military police – the 'redcaps'.

———— ⟨⟩ ————

The fugitive confessed to being a deserter but claimed he was returning to camp. Fulton let him go. Later, the constable's wife mentioned she had seen a soldier half an hour before who looked exactly like the monocled murderer. Fulton checked his wanted person's files and, sure enough, the face of the deserter he had recently met stared back at him. The chase was on.

Fulton originally pursued Toplis alone, catching up with him in the churchyard at High Hesket. Toplis was waiting for the confrontation. He drew his trusted revolver and pointed it straight at Fulton's forehead. 'If it's Toplis you're after, I'm your man.' As he waved the pistol mockingly, he added a sinister footnote: 'I was forced to shoot that lot and if you go on being a bad lad, I may have to shoot you too.'

Fulton threw down his handcuffs and truncheon and backed away. Toplis retreated too, but still pointed the gun at the terrified policeman. Then cheekily

he waved. 'You must be the smartest lawman in England.' He turned and set off on the run again.

Fulton returned in the evening twilight, now armed and accompanied by his colleagues from the local force, with instructions direct from Scotland Yard. Percy Toplis was a big fish. They reached him again as he neared the church of St John the Evangelist, Plumpton. Fulton had an appalling sense of déjà vu. This time, though, the outcome would be very different. As evensong worshippers filed out of the church, Toplis began shooting. In fact, the exchange with the police coalesced into a single cacophony of noise so that nobody could tell who was firing. Toplis clutched his side and fell forward, rolling into a ditch. Inspector Ritchie reached him first, holding him tight as blood and life left Britain's most wanted fugitive. The man with the famous monocle had been just 23 years old and it had taken the murder of a man in Salisbury to bring him down.

BIBLIOGRAPHY

Allison, W. and J. Fairley, *The Monocled Mutineer* (London: Quartet Books, 1979)

Chandler, J. H., *Endless Street: History of Salisbury and its People* (Chichester: Hobnob Press, 1983)

Cave-Penney, H., *The Archaeology of Wiltshire's Towns: An Extensive Urban Survey: Salisbury* (Trowbridge: Wiltshire County Archaeology Service, 2004)

Hatcher, H., *An Historical or Descriptive Account of Old and New Sarum, or Salisbury* (Salisbury: K. Clapperton, 1834)

Thomas, J., *Understanding the Neolithic* (London: Routledge, 1999)

Underwood, P., *Ghosts of Wiltshire* (Bodmin: Bossiney Books, 1989)

Vaughan, D.J., *The Secret Life of Celestina Sommer – A Very Victorian Murder* (2014, e-book available through www. davidjvaughan.co.uk)

Victoria County History series – in particular, *Wiltshire Vol. 3* (ed. Pugh, R.B. and E. Crittall) and *Vol. 6* (ed. Crittall, E.)

White, G., *Bell's Cathedrals: The Cathedral Church of Salisbury. A Description of its Fabric and a Brief History of the See of Sarum* (London: George Bell & Sons, 1898)

Wiltshire Archaeological and Natural History Society, *Wiltshire Archaeological and Natural History Society Magazine* (Devizes: WANHS)

Wiltshire County Archaeology Service, The *Archaeology of Wiltshire's Towns. An Extensive Urban Survey. Old Sarum & Sorviodunum* (Trowbridge: WCAS, 2005)

Wise, S., *Inconvenient People: Lunacy, Liberty and the Mad-Doctors in Victorian England* (London: Vintage, 2013)

Main Image Sources

Wiltshire and Swindon History Centre, Chippenham, Wiltshire (WSHC)

Salisbury and South Wiltshire Museum, Salisbury, Wiltshire

Thomas Fisher Rare Book Library, Library of Toronto (link.library.utoronto.ca/hollar/)

Library of Congress (www.loc.gov/pictures)

Wiltshire Archaeology & Natural History Magazine (WAHMS)

Visit our website and discover thousands of other History Press books.

www.thehistorypress.co.uk